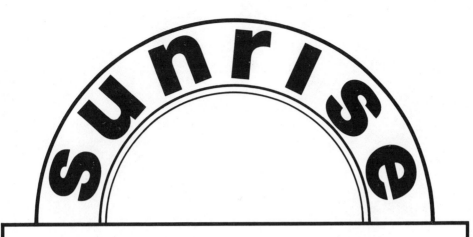

Sunrise

A Breakfast Cookbook
Using Natural Foods
And Whole Grains

By Diana Scesny Greene

THE CROSSING PRESS / TRUMANSBURG, NEW YORK 14886

Copyright © 1980 by Diana Scesny Greene

Cover and book design by Mary A. Scott
Illustrations by Joanne Leary

Printed in the U.S.A.

Library of Congress Cataloging in Publication Data

Greene, Diana Scesny.
    Sunrise, a breakfast cookbook using natural
foods & whole grains.

    Includes bibliographical references and index.
    1. Breakfasts.   2. Cookery (Natural foods).
I.   Title.
TX733.G73   641.5'637   80-20749
ISBN 0-89594-039-6
ISBN 0-89594-040-X (pbk.)

for Jack with love

Contents

Introduction

To eat simply, sanely, and well. These should be the goals of every meal, at every hour. We all know that breakfast "should" be our most nutrition packed meal, but somehow we can't seem to make that happen. Hurried schedules and inveterate habits of a post-noon major meal have reduced the American breakfast to a token repast. Even conscientious homemakers rely on pre-packaged cereals for the one meal that will not stand for such compromise.

Look at it this way. Breakfast is our fuel for the day. Clarity of mind, an optimistic outlook, a bounce to the body. These are all a measure of what gets spooned into the morning bowl. The easiest solution to the breakfast dilemma would probably be a version of the old farm breakfast, which included eggs, milk, meat and cereal grains. Few of us expend the energy necessary to burn up that many calories, however. Further, in an age of resource conservation, many are opposed to the widespread consumption of animal proteins, particularly meat. Finally, who has time to eat or prepare such a breakfast? Those of us with deadlines to meet and goals to achieve need another alternative.

Cereals can be the answer, but not the kind on the supermarket shelf. The statistics are in, and the conclusions are clear. Refined, heated, treated, and sugar coated grains will not keep the sparkle in waking eyes. Liquid protein drinks, while convenient and high in amino acids, aren't the best solution either, because they lack all important fiber. Remember the goals? Simply, sanely and well? Make your own cereals and breakfast foods from whole grains and see what a well-balanced morning meal can do for your day.

In preparing cereal grains there are several things to keep in mind. Most important is the protein complement factor. Although grains are only between 7% and 15% protein on the average, some, such as brown rice, rank higher than meat in terms of their protein usability. For this reason, grains are a good source of protein, especially when complemented by milk, nuts and/or seeds. One third cup of hard red spring wheat provides up to 15% of the daily adult protein requirement, and this is increased up to 3% by the addition of milk, which supplies abundant protein in its own right.[1] One cup of milk, whether whole, skim, or buttermilk, contains 9 grams of protein, or 20% of the daily requirement.[2] Sunflower seeds add approximately 2.5 grams of protein per tablespoon.[3] A medium sized bowl of wheat cereal with a half cup of milk plus a sprinkling of seeds meets almost 30% of the body's protein needs. It wouldn't be difficult to tilt the balance in favor of breakfast by adding a tablespoon of wheat germ or soy grits.

The recipes in this book are all based on the principles of complementary proteins with an eye to maximizing vitamin and mineral content. To boost our reserves of potassium and other minerals, fruits, fresh or dried, are an integral part of each recipe. One-half cup of raisins, for example, provides 2.8 mg. iron, 50 mg. calcium, 112 mg. phosphorus, 575 mg. potassium, and a low 19 mg. sodium.[4] Dates, figs, and apricots are all excellent sources of potassium. An attempt has been made to keep the sodium level low. Kelp, with its high iodine content, usually substitutes for salt, but when kelp does not blend well with the ingredients and salt is called for, it is sea salt, and then only in minor amounts. Nuts and seeds add essential fatty acids.

It is always amazing to learn how many people think that whole grain foods must taste terrible. The very opposite is true. There is such variety and range of texture and taste in cereal grains, that even those with lingering nightmares of the glue-like oatmeal of their youth will find a combination to their liking. Food is supposed to taste good, to be enjoyed. It should appeal to all the senses. There is nothing worse than eating something that looks unappetizing and

---

[1] Frances Moore Lappe, *Diet for a Small Planet*, p. 106.

[2] *Ibid.*, p. 99.

[3] *Ibid.*, p. 104.

[4] Adelle Davis, *Let's Eat Right To Keep Fit*, pp. 292-293.

tastes worse solely because it is supposed to be "good for you." That kind of eating will never result in a harmony of mind and body.

Remember: grain plus a milk product plus fruit and nuts. Always keep the balance and do not skimp on any one, because it will alter the protein composition as well as the taste. Vary the ingredients to suit your individual preferences, but be sure that the end result is delicious. Serve the cereals complete and be seasonal in the choice. "Mush-On!" can get a bleak January morning off to a warm and comfortable start, but it won't fit the bill in the middle of June. Then it's time for a cool crunchy granola with fresh fruit and a glass of frosty yogurt nog.

Recommended cooking methods preserve the nutrients as much as possible. Since all of these recipes were devised and tested with the use of a wood cookstove, ideal textures and consistencies were easy to achieve. Whole grains can be temperamental; their absorption rates vary with the temperature at which they are added to the liquid and subsequently cooked. Some cereals, like rolled oats, cook best in water, while corn meal in milk gives an outstanding performance. Though almost any cereal can be eaten in any stage of cooking, the starting and cooking temperatures *do* make a difference in the end product. For a morning meal with eye appeal, tune in to the nuances of the grain, and give it what it needs to give you its best. All of the cereals in this book can be cooked directly on an electric range or over a gas flame. The cooking times given are for *low* heat, preferably to the side of a wood range or heater. The same effect can be achieved by a double boiler, although this is not necessary to cook a good cereal.

Most nutrition boosters, like wheat germ, bran, seeds and nuts, should be added toward the end of the cooking time for hot cereal. The object of cooking at all is to remove the raw taste of the germ or bran, and this is accomplished within a few minutes. More prolonged cooking destroys nutrients. Pumpkin or sunflower seeds, likewise, need only to be warmed. The exceptions are sesame seeds and chopped peanuts, which should be lightly roasted ahead of time for the fullest flavor. Soy grits must be cooked with the cereal.

The addition of fruits to any cereal, hot or cold, is a matter of taste and texture. Raisins added to the boiling water of oatmeal give a sweeter taste to the cereal, while they lose much of their individual taste. When added a few minutes before serving and "steamed" on top of the cereal, which plumps them, the raisins keep their distinctive flavor to themselves. Then it's a matter of full oat flavor dotted with chewy raisins. The raisin water flavor clearly does not complement some cereals, so its always best to try the steam method first. If the taste agrees, then try it with the cooking water. When cooking a cream cereal, dried fruits can curdle the milk unless added last, after the cereal is done cooking. Use common sense and then follow your taste buds.

Granola, the general name given to a variety of cold mixed grain cereals, also responds to differing oven conditions. A wood stove, for example, produces a more golden hue than an electric oven. For every recipe, it is recommended that oven temperature does not exceed 350 degrees. That is an upper limit. The lower the temperature, the longer it will take the granola to crisp, but fewer nutrients will be lost in the process. In all cases, check the granola periodically and keep a metal (stainless steel) spatula handy to turn the cereal along the edges in toward the center so that an evenly browned cereal results. The edges always brown first and can scorch unless the cereal is "rotated" on the cookie sheet. Much has been said about cookware these days, and with all the turning and scraping in the making of granola, I feel safer using stainless steel. Since granolas call for an acid ingredient of some kind—honey, molasses or maple syrup—these cereals can react with aluminum, which is, after all, a heavy metal. Several points to remember when making granola: do not boil the honey before adding, since high heat destroys the enzymes, and do not add dried fruit to the unbaked cereal. Raisins, in particular, will scorch long before the granola is ready. Another lesson learned by experience: if you like your granola crunchy, don't add the dried fruits until the cereal is in your breakfast bowl. When left to stand together, the cereal will absorb the available moisture in the fruit and lose its crunch. For those who like a chewier cereal, this would be an ideal way of achieving it.

If it all sounds like too much to remember, don't be discouraged. Making your own cereals is as much a matter of routine and organization as whatever else you're doing in the morning. All of these cereals can, and should be, prepared ahead of time in their dry state and stored, in quantity, in the refrigerator or other cool place. Then, come morning, it's only a matter of taking hold of the measuring cup and the cereal pot (a heavy duty saucepan and lid, such as Farberware, which distributes bottom heat evenly.) The cereal cooks itself, while you get ready for the day. Keep a special section of the refrigerator reserved for the cereal condiments—butter, milk products, syrup, seeds, dried fruits—so that they can all be brought to the table in a minimum of movements. It won't be long before getting a good breakfast takes no more time than reaching for a bad breakfast from the supermarket shelf.

Throughout the book I refer to milk products. By that I mean fresh milk, whole or skim, powdered milk, instant or non-instant, evaporated milk, canned whole milk, or yogurt, whole or skim. Any milk product that does not have sugar added, such as condensed milk, will do. The aim of adding milk is to complement the cereal protein and increase the overall protein content of the meal. It can't be left out, so experiment until you find a kind of milk to your liking. Ideally, the milk should be eaten with the cereal so that they are available to the body's digestive system at the same time. For those who insist upon eating cereals plain or dry, a glass of hot or cold milk with the breakfast will serve the same purpose. Don't overlook yogurt as a milk product. It goes great on hot cereal and cold, as well as pancakes and muffins. Make yogurt the main feature of some mornings, with a generous sprinkling of granola and fresh fruit on the top. Or try toasted wheat germ, bananas and maple syrup. As long as you choose from a basic list of ingredients and always be sure to complement, any cereal creation will be nutritious, so it's only a matter of what appeals to you personally. These recipes are only a beginning.

Maple syrup, honey and molasses should be the only sweeteners allowed on the breakfast table. Molasses is rich in potassium, calcium, phosphorus, iron, thiamine, riboflavin and niacin. Honey contains the same minerals and vitamins, except thiamine, in lesser quantities, but has the added advantage of enzymes. Maple sugar has lost its vitamins in the long process of boiling it down, but remains a good source of calcium, phosphorus, iron and potassium. Of the three, honey is the lowest in sodium.[5]

Cereal breakfasts can be as varied as the days of the week or as festive as the coming season. Pancakes, which require more time in preparation, are good weekend specials for late morning breakfasts that stay with you until dinnertime. Since they require eggs and milk, pancakes are a natural for getting high protein. However, since the grains are not cooked in the liquid, it takes more flour to make pancakes and consequently more calories per serving. Let the choice of

---

[5]"Composition of Foods," Agriculture Handbook, No. 8, USDA.

pancakes correspond to your energy needs for the day, and be creative. Spoon yogurt on top of the stack and just drizzle the syrup over it to keep calories down and protein up.

Breads by themselves are often not high enough in protein to stand alone as breakfast foods. I have included several recipes for special occasions either to accompany eggs or to be served with a glass of yogurt nog. The breads combine the complementary proteins of wheat and milk and all get a nutritional boost from the addition of eggs. Fruited and nut rolled breakfast breads give a head start on meeting the day's mineral requirements.

A book of all cereals or all pancakes and breakfast breads would be a book without end. *Sunrise* is merely a book of suggestions to reintroduce you to morning and the thousands of possibilities that it holds. Be certain of what you are giving your body, and your body will be certain to repay you well for the effort. Make your own breakfast. Simply, sanely, and well.

Grain Mills and Flour

Most whole grain flours are now available through health food stores, co-ops and wholesale distributors of natural foods. There are several drawbacks to such commercially milled flours. When flours are steel ground in large quantity and at high speed, the temperatures produced in milling cause a deterioration of the heat sensitive vitamins, particularly of the B group. Both steel and stone ground flours are also susceptible to the same nutritional losses due to the time that elapses between milling, packaging and marketing. The germ particles, whether of wheat, corn or oats, begin to oxidize upon contact with the air, and the longer it takes to get the flour from the mill to the table, the greater are the chances for the germ to go rancid. Like any rancid oil, aged wheat germ increases the body's requirement for vitamin E, causing a chain reaction of unfavorable events.[6] There is also little, if any, choice of fineness in the grind among commercially milled flours, and many of the less requested flours, such as soy and

---

[6] Adelle Davis, *Let's Eat Right To Keep Fit,* p. 47.

rice, are extremely powdery. With corn, on the other hand, coarseness seems to be the rule. Full fat soy flour is often difficult to find. In short, go ahead and purchase your whole grain flours only if you are sure of the source and satisfied with the grind, but regard these products as merely the first stage in your culinary career. The full range of whole grain flavors and textures can be experienced only when you mill the grain yourself.

The advantages of owning your own grain mill are numerous. Grains and legumes may be purchased in bulk and stored whole. If cool and free of moisture, they will keep almost indefinitely in this state. Flours can then be ground upon demand. I also grind ahead and freeze enough hard wheat flour to make one batch of Basic Whole Wheat Dough and enough pastry wheat flour for several batches of pancakes in case the temperature drops to -50 and I can't get to the grain mill. Each breakfast cook will have her/his separate reason for keeping a small reserve of ground flour, but be sure these flours are kept under refrigeration or frozen to preserve nutrients. You may also want to have a few cups of soy flour on hand, so it will be easily accessible for adding to any recipe. The specialty flours—brown rice, buckwheat, garbanzo, peanut—should probably be ground fresh.

The type of mill you purchase will determine to a large extent how much flour you will want to pre-grind and how much you should grind upon demand. Grain mills present a hierarchy of compromises, and you must choose the one that offers the most appropriate compromise for your situation. There has been a long standing debate over the merits of stone ground flour versus steel ground. Stone mill enthusiasts claim that the heat generated by steel burrs causes nutritional damage to the grain. On the other hand, stone mills are difficult to turn by hand, and the use of motors to turn the stones results in increased milling speed and, in turn, greater friction and heat. Heat then being equal, the other issues to consider are volume and versatility. How much flour will you be grinding in a year? Is electricity available? Finally, will you be grinding soybeans, peanuts, nuts, or seeds?

Flour milling should be a joy, not an ordeal. The simplest and most versatile mill is the Corona steel mill, to which I refer repeatedly in this book. It is inexpensive, hand operated, and will grind everything from hard wheat flour to peanut butter. Further, it can be cleaned. While I have another larger steel mill, A Diamant, for quantity milling, the Corona is indispensable for a quick cup of corn meal, rice flour or whole bean soy. While the grain must be run through the mill several times, this repeat process, during which the steel plates are brought closer together, makes it easy to obtain the optimum texture for every cooking purpose. In general, steel mills produce the best cracked grains for hot cereals, since the burrs cut cleanly and do not produce an abundance of fine powdery particles as stone mills do. Two passes for soft wheat produce a fine pastry flour, while three for hard wheat yield quality bread flour. However, hand operated steel mills are undeniably work and they rarely produce the quantities of flour in the times stated in their manuals. I do not have electricity and happen to enjoy the exercise of grinding grain and the satisfaction gained from maximum involvement with the foods I prepare and serve. If you have neither the time nor the inclination to turn a steel wheel, by all means buy an electric mill. In this case, you may want to consider stones.

Stone mills produce extremely fine flour in one pass. Since most are motor driven, they are effortless and turn out large quantities in minutes. Yeast doughs made from stone ground wheat are remarkably light. With the exception of the Marathon Mill, however, stone wheels cannot be used with oily foods, such as soybeans, peanuts or sunflower seeds. There are also milling stones on the market that slough off annoying amounts of grit, so investigate the model and manufacturer thoroughly. Should you choose a stone mill, the Corona would be a good back up mill for cracked grains and oily seeds and beans.

Porridges Hot

Whole Grain Cereals

Cereals made with whole grains that are uncut and uncracked are the most interesting from a texture standpoint, but because of long cooking times they are prepared the least frequently of all. A little forethought and a few short cuts can make these cereals a regular feature of the breakfast menu.

Mixed Berry Cereal

This recipe yields enough cereal for four servings. That means two mornings for two! Wheat berries, as well as rye and triticale, reheat well. In fact, the cereal can even be frozen in breakfast sized quantities, then thawed the night before serving. That way, the cereal becomes a quick meal.

2/3 c. hard wheat berries
2/3 c. rye berries
3 c. cold water

1. 24 hours before serving, soak wheat berries and rye berries in cold water. Cover.
2. That evening boil the berries in the soaking water with 1/2 tsp. salt for 5 minutes. Pour, with liquid, into a quart size wide mouth stainless steel thermos. The cereal will be ready to eat the following morning.
3. Serve with butter, milk product, maple syrup, honey or pepper.

If your thermos does not keep the cereal piping hot, pour the cereal into a sauce pan and bring the berries and liquid to a quick boil. If the berries have absorbed all the water overnight, add a small quantity of boiling water when reheating.

This cereal does not need a sweetener to enhance the flavor, and makes a lively morning dish when liberally dashed with freshly ground pepper. By the same token, it can double as a main meal feature. Try serving the leftover portion mixed with cheese, garlic, and preferred spices.

Variations
1. Substitute brown rice for the rye berries
2. Use all whole wheat, triticale, wild rice or kasha.
3. Add raisins when you are boiling the berries.

Dutch Barley Cereal

1/2 c. barley (pearled)
2 c. water
1/4 tsp. sea salt
1 chopped or grated raw apple
2-3 T. raisins
2 T. honey

1. 24 hours before serving, soak the barley in the water.
2. The next morning bring the barley and soaking water to a boil and add the salt. Simmer 45 minutes, covered.
3. Stir in the raw apple, raisins and honey. Steam an additional 15 minutes.
4. Serve with double milk, sprinkling of lecithin granules, (additional honey)* and (sunflower seeds).

DOUBLE MILK

Double milk is just what the name implies: twice the regular amount of milk solids to the regular measure of liquid. To make double milk from fresh milk, add 1/3 c. powdered instant to each cup liquid. Using all powdered milk, add 2/3 cup instant to each cup water. Evaporated whole milk or evaporated skim milk are already double and can be used straight from the can. Since carob lacks the fat content of cocoa, the double milk gives this cereal its "hot chocolate" taste.

---

* The parentheses indicates item is optional.

Rice Pudding Cereal

1 c. plus 2 T. water
1/4 tsp. sea salt
1/2 c. short grain brown rice
1/4 c. raisins
2 T. honey
1 c. boiling water
2/3 c. instant powdered milk
     or
1 c. whole milk plus 1/3 c. powdered

1. Bring the water and the sea salt to a boil. Without stirring, add rice. Resume boil, cover, and simmer for 30 minutes or until the water is absorbed. The amount of water will have to be increased slightly for long grain rice.
2. Stir in the raisins, honey, boiling water and milk. You may use whole milk plus powdered milk in place of the water and powdered milk. Simmer 15-20 minutes. Do not allow the milk to come to a full boil or it will curdle. Stir and serve with lecithin granules, cinnamon or sunflower seeds.

LECITHIN GRANULES

Lecithin granules are usually added after the cooking period. While they are mild flavored, they do have a taste of their own which comes out more emphatically when cooked along with the cereal. In more delicately flavored cereals, such as Rice Pudding Cereal, adding the lecithin granules on top of the cooked cereal to be stirred in just before eating minimizes flavor interference.

Cracked Grain Cereals

Grains for the following cereals are all prepared by running the whole berries through a steel or stone mill set for very coarse grind. The resulting particles should measure approximately 1/8th inch to 3/16th inch across. Once cracked, the cereal should be refrigerated until used to protect oils in the germ.

Cracked Wheat Cereal
(Basic)

2 c. water
1/2 tsp. kelp
1/4 c. raisins
1/2 c. cracked hard red wheat
2 T. sunflower seeds
(2 tsp. lecithin granules)

1. Bring to a boil the water, kelp and raisins. Add the wheat slowly while stirring. Simmer, covered, for 15-20 minutes, until liquid is absorbed and the grain is tender.
2. Add the sunflower seeds and lecithin (optional) during last few minutes of cooking.
3. Serve with butter, milk product, (maple syrup—some may find wheat sweet enough by itself) and cinnamon.

Cracked Rye Wheat Cereal

2 c. water
1/2 tsp. kelp
1/4 c. raisins
1/4 c. cracked rye
1/4 c. cracked hard red wheat

1. Bring to a boil the water, kelp and raisins. Add the rye and wheat, stirring as you go.
2. Prepare and serve the same as for Cracked Wheat Cereal.

Triple Grain Cereal

2 T. cracked rye
2 T. cracked oats (steel cut)
1/2 c. (minus 4 T.) cracked hard wheat
2 c. water
1/2 tsp. kelp
1/4 c. raisins
1/2 c. mixed cracked grains
2 T. sunflower seeds
(2 tsp. lecithin granules)

1. Measure the rye and oats into a half-cup measure. Fill until level with the wheat.
2. Bring to a boil the water, kelp and raisins. Stir in the cracked grains. Resume boil, cover, reduce heat and simmer for 15-20 minutes.
3. Add the sunflower seeds and lecithin (optional). Steam 3-5 minutes. Stir.
4. Serve with butter, milk product and (maple syrup).

Steel cut oats and cracked oats are practically interchangeable. Commercially cut oats are sold as "steel cut" because they are passed through steel blades, while home cut oats can be cracked in either a steel or stone mill. Texture varies depending upon the company selling the product; some steel cut oats tend to be extremely coarse, thus requiring longer cooking. When oats are cracked at home, the resulting product tends to have a higher percentage of finer particles, which make the cooked cereals creamier. If you crack your own grain, adjust the setting on the mill so that no particles are larger than 1/3 the size of a whole oat berry. If particles are larger than this, the cereal will not absorb moisture uniformly and may stick to the bottom of the saucepan when cooking.

Cracked Oat Cereal
(Basic)

2 c. water
1 tsp. kelp
1/4 c. raisins or cut up figs
1/2 c. steel cut or cracked oats
2 T. sunflower seeds
(1 tsp. lecithin)

1. Bring to a boil the water, kelp and raisins (or figs). While stirring, add the oats. Bring to a boil, cover, reduce heat and continue cooking over low heat for 15-20 minutes, depending on the coarseness of the grain.
2. Sprinkle the sunflower seeds (and lecithin) on top. Steam for an additional 2-3 minutes. Stir.
3. Serve with butter, cinnamon, maple syrup and milk product.

Coconoat Cereal

This cereal is an excellent way to start the family on home-made breakfasts. The sweet dessert blend of dates and coconut is especially appealing to children.

2 c. water
1/2 tsp. kelp
1/2 c. cracked oats
2-3 T. unsweetened grated coconut
1/3 c. chopped dates
2 T. sunflower seeds

1. Bring to a boil the water and kelp. Stir in the oats and coconut. Bring to a second boil, cover, reduce heat and simmer for 15 minutes.
2. Add the dates and sunflower seeds without stirring. Steam for 5 minutes. Stir.
3. Serve with milk product, (butter), (syrup or honey), (lecithin granules).

Pecan Oat Cereal

Pecan meal can be purchased from Southern pecan growers at a cost considerably lower than whole nuts. If you are making your own meal in large quantities, however, frozen nuts can be ground through a Corona steel mill or blender or chopped finely with a hand chopper. Since pecans are a soft nut, it is just as easy to chop up a week's worth by hand.

2 c. water
1/2 tsp. kelp
1/2 c. cracked oats
2 T. pecan meal
1/4 c. chopped dried papaya
1 tsp. lecithin granules

1. Bring to a boil the water and kelp. Stir in the oats and pecan meal. Return to a boil, cover, reduce heat and simmer over low flame for 15 minutes.
2. Add the papaya and lecithin on top. Steam an additional 5 minutes. Stir.
3. Serve with butter, milk product, maple syrup and nutmeg.

Carob Almond Cereal

Although carob lacks the fat content of cocoa, double milk served on this cereal gives it a "hot chocolate" taste.

2 c. water
1/2 tsp. kelp
1/2 c. cracked oats
2 T. carob flour
2 T. raw peanut meal
1-2 T. chopped raw almonds
2 T. honey
1/4 c. raisins
1/2 tsp. cinnamon

1. Bring to a boil the water and kelp. Add, with a whisk, the oats, carob and peanut meal. Return to a boil, cover, and simmer over lowest heat for 15 minutes.
2. Stir in the almonds, honey, raisins and cinnamon. Return to low heat and simmer 2-3 minutes. Stir.
3. Serve with (butter), double milk* or cream, (additional honey).

Oat Porridge

2 c. water
1/2 tsp. kelp
1/3 c. cracked oats
2 T. raw peanut meal
3 T. raw wheat germ

1. Bring to a boil the water and kelp. Stir in the oats and peanut meal. Return to a boil, cover, reduce heat and simmer 15 minutes.
2. Stir in the wheat germ. Steam for 5 minutes. Stir.
3. Serve with butter, milk product, (sunflower seeds), (maple syrup), (lecithin granules).

---

*See page 4 for instructions on how to make double milk.

The hull on mature buckwheat is extremely tough and does not soften with cooking. Buckwheat purchased as kasha has the dark husk removed and cracking presents no problem. Simply grind the groats through a stone or steel mill at the setting necessary to yield particles approximately one third the size of the whole kernel. If the buckwheat is unhulled, however, follow this procedure: crack the whole buckwheat coarsely in a grain mill, then sift through a wire mesh strainer or flour sifter. The hull readily separates from the groat in grinding, and the larger particles are easily caught by the sifting. Some dark pieces of husk will remain in the cereal, but these will be fine enough to cause no problem in texture.

Buckwheat by itself makes too pasty a cereal. Best results are achieved by combining it with other grains in proportion such that the buckwheat does not exceed one half the total of cereal grains.

Buck Wheat Cereal

2 c. water
1/4 tsp. sea salt or 1 tsp. kelp
1/4 c. cracked hard wheat
1/4 c. cracked buckwheat, raw or toasted
1 T. lecithin
1/4 c. raisins
2 T. raw hulled sunflower seeds

1. Bring to a boil the water, sea salt or kelp. Stir in the wheat and buckwheat. Return to a boil, cover and reduce heat. Simmer for 15-20 minutes on lowest setting possible.
2. Add on top, without stirring, the lecithin, raisins and sunflower seeds. Steam an additional 2-3 minutes. Stir.
3. Serve with butter, milk product, (maple syrup).

Cream Cereals

Any cereal grain can be turned into a cream cereal. The grain need only be toasted ahead of time, then ground into fine particles in a steel or stone mill. Starting with a cold dry cast iron skillet, cover the bottom with a layer of whole berries or kernels. Stir constantly over medium heat until browned. Berries and rice grains may "pop," but do not be alarmed. Such popped or parched wheat is a snack all by itself. Transfer the toasted grain to a bowl and let cool thoroughly. Then grind in a grain mill on a setting for meal. If the cereal is ground too fine, the cooked cereal will be pasty.

Cream of Wheat
(Basic)

2 c. water
2/3 c. powdered milk (instant)
1/4 tsp. sea salt
1/2 c. toasted, ground hard red spring wheat
1/4 c. raisins
2 T. sunflower seeds

1. Bring to a simmer the water, powdered milk and salt. Whisk in the wheat. Bring to a boil, stirring constantly, then simmer, covered, for 15 minutes.
2. Sprinkle the raisins and sunflower seeds on top. Steam for an additional 2-3 minutes. Stir.
3. Serve with a sprinkling of lecithin granules, butter, milk product, (maple syrup), (cinnamon).

Cream of Rice

Prepare as for Cream of Wheat, substituting 1/2 c. ground parched brown rice for the wheat. In place of sunflower seeds try toasted sesame seeds.

Creamy Rice Wheat Cereal

Measure 2 T. ground toasted rice into a 1/2 c. measuring cup. Fill to the top with ground toasted wheat. Prepare and serve the cereal as for Cream of Wheat.

Cream cereals made from corn call for coarsely ground unroasted corn of the field variety. However, dried corn can be parched in the oven (dry roasted) for half an hour, then cooled before grinding to produce a somewhat different flavor and texture. Such parched corn, known as "pinole" in the Southwest, can be eaten cold with milk. Roasting cooks the grain, making it easier to chew and digest. As such, "pinole" makes a convenient food for backpackers and hikers.

Corn Cereal
(Basic)

2 c. water
2/3 c. powdered milk
1/4 tsp. sea salt
1/2 c. coarse corn meal (white or yellow)
1/4 c. chopped pitted dates
2 T. raw hulled pumpkin seeds

1. Bring water, milk and salt to a simmer. Do not boil. Whisk in the corn meal. Bring ingredients to a boil, whisking constantly to prevent scorching; then simmer, covered, over lowest heat.
2. Sprinkle the dates and pumpkin seeds on top. Let cereal steam for 2-3 minutes. Stir.
3. Serve with butter or peanut butter, milk product and maple syrup, honey or molasses.

Broken cashews or chopped dry roasted peanuts make an interesting substitute for the pumpkin seeds. Cashews can be added raw. The peanuts should be roasted ahead of time for full flavor. This is done by spreading a thin layer, about two nuts high, in a baking pan and roasting the nuts in the oven for approximately 30 minutes at 350 degrees. (Roast the peanuts with their red skins on.) Check occasionally for scorching. Shake the pan for more even roasting. Store the roasted nuts in glass jars and keep refrigerated.

In place of butter, try peanut butter (natural), cashew butter or sesame tahini for added protein.

Corn Bran Cereal

2 c. cold water
1/4 c. miller's bran
1/2 c. coarse yellow corn meal
1/4 tsp. sea salt
2 T. raw wheat germ

1. Measure into a saucepan the water, bran, corn meal and salt. Bring ingredients to a boil, whisking throughout, then simmer, covered, for 20 minutes.
2. Stir in the wheat germ. Cook an additional 3-5 minutes. Stir.
3. Serve with butter, maple syrup, milk product.

"Mush-On!" Cereal

This one has to be started the night before.

2 c. water
2/3 c. powdered milk
1/4 tsp. sea salt
1/2 c. coarsely ground white or yellow corn meal

1. Bring to a simmer the water, dry milk and salt. Whisk in the corn meal. Yellow corn meal has more vitamin A. Whisk or stir until the mixture begins to boil, then reduce heat and simmer, covered, for 20 minutes over lowest heat setting.
2. Remove from heat and pour into an oiled square form. (For two people, a pint sized square freezer container works fine.) Chill, covered, overnight.
3. In the morning, invert the form onto a cutting board and cut into 1/2 inch thick slices. Dredge the slices in whole wheat pastry flour or bran. Fry them slowly in safflower oil or a combination of safflower oil and butter, until crisp.
4. Serve as is or with butter and maple syrup.

Fried mush is usually made from a corn and water based cereal. The addition of milk powder, which provides a protein complement to the corn, increases the nutritional value of the cereal. Corn Bran Cereal, see page 16, can also be chilled, sliced and sauteed for a breakfast variation. If time and diet allow, fried mush makes a great base for poached or fried eggs.

Confetti Corn Cereal

1 T. soy grits
1/2 c. minus 1 T. white corn meal
2 c. water
2/3 c. powdered milk
1/4 tsp. sea salt
2 T. raw peanut meal
1/4 c. chopped dates

1. Spoon into a 1/2 cup measure the grits. Fill to the top with corn meal. Set aside.
2. Bring to a simmer the water, powdered milk and salt. Whisk in the grits, corn meal and peanut meal. Bring to a boil, whisking constantly. Then cook, covered, over lowest heat or on top of a double boiler for 15 minutes.
3. Add the dates. Steam an additional 5 minutes. Stir.
4. Serve with butter, maple syrup, milk product and a sprinkling of lecithin.

There's a standing debate between Southerners and Northerners over the comparative taste merits of white and yellow corn meals. In this cereal, we side with the South: there's something about the white corn that makes the combination of flavors a hard one to beat. The vitamin A lacking in white meal is more than compensated by A-rich dates.

RAW PEANUT MEAL

Raw peanut meal can be made in a variety of ways. Spanish peanuts, the most readily available raw hulled peanuts, should be processed with the skins, or papers, on. If you have a Corona steel mill, freeze the peanuts and then feed them through the mill as you would any grain. Adjust the setting so that the peanuts come out as crumbly flakes which quickly break apart to form a coarse meal. The freezing keeps the oiliness to a minimum and makes the mill easier to clean afterward. If you run a small quantity of a hard grain such as wheat through the mill right after the peanuts, you will not have to take the mill apart to clean it. Keep the peanut meal refrigerated at all times.

A blender also does a fine job in making peanut meal. Follow the instructions for making peanut butter or for grinding coffee in your machine. If you follow the directions for peanut butter, do *not* add additional oil, which is usually called for. Simply grind a small quantity of peanuts at a time and empty into a refrigerator container for storage.

A last resort, but by no means an inferior method, is an old fashioned nut chopper. The German made "Blitz" chopper produces a fine grind given enough arm power. Any other nut grinder or chopper will work as well.

The texture you are trying to achieve is that of finely ground nuts. Peanut flour is not the desired texture for cooked cereals. Also, bear in mind that raw peanuts do not have the distinctive peanut flavor, which is a result of roasting the legumes. Rather, the end result in cooked cereals comes closer to ground almonds or hazelnuts. Because of the high protein content of peanuts and their combined presence with milk, peanut meal is an economical nutritional booster in any cereal.

See page 33 for instructions on making peanut butter.

Flaked Cereals

Cereal flakes require more elaborate equipment to produce than most households provide. However, flakes are gaining in popularity and can be readily purchased in health food stores as well as supermarkets. Rolled oats are basically a flaked cereal and can be purchased almost anywhere. Always look for "old-fashioned" oats, which means that they have not been pre-processed (heat treated) for fast cooking. Regular rolled oats cook fast enough and retain more of their original nutrients.

Since the flaking or rolling process disturbs the bran layer and exposes the germ oils to air, cereal flakes should be kept refrigerated. The thickness of the flakes will vary, depending upon the producer, and this thickness will affect cooking time. A thicker flake yields a chewier cereal and possibly will require slightly more liquid.

Flakes absorb water more readily than milk and cook more quickly if simply added to seasoned water. Milk solids, instant or non-instant, should be stirred in after the flakes are tender. Dried fruits cooked with the flakes will plump up and lend their distinctive flavors to the various grains. Flakes can also be cooked in fruit juices, such as apple, orange or pineapple.

Any flake—wheat, rye, triticale or barley—can be substituted for the rolled oats in the following recipes. Try using sorghum as a sweetener with these distinctively flavored grains.

Oatmeal
(Basic)

2 c. water
1/2 tsp. kelp
1/4 c. raisins
1 c. rolled oats
2 T. sunflower seeds
1 tsp. lecithin granules

1. Bring to a boil the water, kelp and raisins. Add the oats while stirring. Return to a boil, cover, reduce heat and simmer for 15 minutes.
2. Stir in the sunflower seeds and the lecithin. Steam 2-3 minutes. Stir.
3. Serve with butter, peanut butter or cashew butter, double milk or yogurt, maple syrup and cinnamon.

   If substituting 1/4 c. chopped pitted dates for the raisins, add them at the same time as the sunflower seeds, *i.e.,* after the flakes are tender.

Oatmeal Boost

   Prepare as for Basic Oatmeal, but stir in 1/3 c. powdered milk when the sunflower seeds are added.

Bran Oat Cereal

2 c. water
1/2 tsp. kelp
1/4 c. raisins
1/2 c. bran flakes (miller's bran)
1/2 c. rolled oats
1/4 c. raw wheat germ
2 T. sunflower seeds

1. Bring to a boil the water, kelp and raisins. Stir in the bran and oats. Return to a boil, cover, reduce heat and simmer for 15 minutes.
2. Stir in the wheat germ and sunflower seeds. Steam 3-5 minutes, just long enough to get the raw flavor out of the wheat germ. Stir.
3. Serve with butter, maple syrup, milk product, cinnamon or allspice and a sprinkling of lecithin granules.

Apricot Oat Cereal

2 1/2 c. water
1/4 c. chopped dried apricots (up to 12 halves)
1/2 tsp. kelp
1 c. rolled oats
2 T. raw wheat germ
2 T. raw cashew pieces
2 T. honey

1. Bring to a boil the water, apricots and kelp. Stir in the oats. Resume boil, cover, reduce heat and simmer for 10-15 minutes.
2. Stir in the wheat germ, cashews and honey. Steam 3-5 more minutes. Stir.
3. Serve with (butter), milk product, additional honey or syrup and a sprinkling of lecithin granules.

✻Cinnamon Apple Cereal

2 c. water
1/2 tsp. kelp
1/2 tsp. cinnamon
1 c. rolled oats
1/2 grated raw apple, washed and cored but unpeeled
2 T. sunflower seeds
1 tsp. lecithin granules

1. Bring to a boil the water, kelp and cinnamon. Stir in the oats.
Return to a boil, cover, reduce heat and simmer for 15 minutes.
2. Stir in the apple, sunflower seeds and lecithin. Steam for 5 minutes. Stir.
3. Serve with butter, maple syrup or honey and a milk product.

Variations
1. Substitute up to 2 c. apple juice for the cooking water.
2. Add 1/2 c. thick unsweetened applesauce to cooked cereal instead of grated apple.
3. Use 1/4-1/3 c. chopped dehydrated apples, adding to the cooking water, which should be increased by 1/3-1/2 c.

Aloha Oats Cereal

This makes a mildly pineapple flavored cereal.

2 1/4 c. water
1/2 tsp. kelp
1/3 c. chopped dried pineapple
1 c. rolled oats
3 T. grated unsweetened coconut
2 T. honey

1. Bring to a boil the water, kelp and pineapple. Stir in the oats, coconut and honey. Resume boil, cover, reduce heat and simmer for 15 minutes. Stir.
2. Serve with milk product and additional honey.

Variations
1. Use canned crushed pineapple instead of dried, reducing the water to 2 c. and adding pineapple after the oats are tender (15 minutes).
2. Substitute one cup or more of unsweetened pineapple juice for the cooking water.

Cereals with a Crunch

Variations
on
The Theme of Granola

Granola

Granolas are the ultimate challenge and delight of the breakfast cook. The variables are endless: the grains can be floured, powdered or flaked; the nuts might be ground, shredded, chopped, roasted or raw; fruit can be added or not, depending on individual preference.

Granola is basically a multi-ingredient cereal mixed for eating dry or with milk, yogurt or any other milk product, including nut and soy milks. The Swiss "Familia" or "Muesli," a rolled oat, wheat, rye and almond combination, was a forerunner in the present granola explosion. The cereal was sweetened by the addition of raw sugar, and, since it lacked the adhesive qualities of honey and oil, was free pouring.

American tastes tend toward more crunch. Therefore oil and/or butter are added which, when poured over the cereal flakes and other dry ingredients and baked, gives granola the desired crunch. At the same time, the moistening requires longer cooking time in the oven so that the cereal, which has absorbed the honey and oil, can roast under cover of this coating. When recipes simply call for dry roasting of the basic grains used in the granola mix without the addition of honey and oil, the resulting cereal will be initially crisp when the cereal is poured into the breakfast bowl, but will quickly become soggy when milk is added (similar to the original "Muesli"). Honeyed and oiled grains, on the other hand, retain their crunch through to the last spoonful.

Individual preferences will ultimately influence each person's list of ingredients. Fruited granolas are very popular but require several precautions. If the dried fruits are added before the cereal flakes are toasted, they are likely to scorch unless the oven is set at an extremely low heat. Yet at such a low heat setting, perhaps 225 degrees F., the cereal flakes do not get very crispy, and the end product is a compromise. If the fruits are added after the rest of the ingredients have crisped, they tend to impart moisture to the roasted ingredients during storage and produce another equally compromised granola. For these reasons I do not recommend adding fruit to the granola mix until the cereal is served, and then individual portions of dried raisins, chopped apricot, pineapple, papaya, or apple or any combination of fresh fruits can be added. The only exception I have made is dates, which do not dry out at an oven setting of 350 degrees F., and fruit purees, such as mashed banana or honey rhubarb, which serve as part of the liquid ingredients and will lose their water content during the baking time. The purees flavor the cereal throughout, so be sure the fruit you use is one that the family particularly enjoys.

The basic principles for cold cereal composition are the same as those for hot cereals. Cereal proteins should be complemented whenever possible by the addition of other cereal grains, nuts, seeds, or milk solids. Usually the granolas are eaten with a minimum of one-half cup milk per serving, but in the event that the cereal will be eaten as a snack or dry for any other reason, try to include milk solids (powdered non-fat milk) among the ingredients. For those who must restrict intake of milk products, granolas make an attractive breakfast choice, since the other ingredients can be proportioned for maximum protein. Wheat germ should be increased as well as seeds such as sunflower and pumpkin. Soy, cashew or sesame milks are all possible liquid replacements for cow's milk. Soy and sesame seeds are a good source of calcium, and so are almonds and brazil nuts, although to a lesser degree.

There is no market substitute for a homemade granola that has been prepared with fresh grains, plump seeds and pure cold-pressed oils. Oats are traditionally the major component of granolas, but wheat and rye flakes alone or in combination make tasty cereals. Wheat germ for extra protein and bran for increased fiber are two important additions and can be adjusted according to individual needs. Milk solids, soy flour and brewer's yeast are other possible nutritional boosters, but both soy and yeast have dominant tastes and should be added only when another equally dominant flavor such as peanut or molasses is present to balance them. Sweeteners, if used, should come from the honey, maple syrup and molasses group to include trace minerals. A combination of oil and butter provides essential fatty acids. **The average ratio of liquid to dry for a crunchy cereal is 5 1/2 cups of dry ingredients to 1 cup liquid.** Usually the liquid component is equally divided between the sweetener and the oil or butter.

Fortunately, oils and butter turn ordinary grains and seeds into delicious crunchy cereals and snacks. However, their inclusion in the granola recipes rests on several nutritional considerations. Fats are important for the maintenance of overall body health, in particular for the well being of the nerves, brain, hormonal system and digestive tract. High protein and high fiber are not enough for good health. Three essential fatty acids must be supplied: linoleic, linolenic and arachidonic acids. Linoleic, which is absolutely vital, is supplied by vegetable oils, nuts and seeds. Safflower oil contains up to 90% of this essential fatty acid, which is also needed for the absorption of vitamins A, D, E, and K.[1]

Dieters who shun oils for caloric reasons should be aware that when fats are undersupplied, the body converts sugar to fat faster than normal. Avoiding all fats actually adds to the weight problem. Similarly, small portions of high fiber foods antagonize the problem. The greater the quantity of bran, the less calories the body will be converting into fat. Wheat bran, in particular, will help the body maintain and regulate its proper weight.[2]

If all the essential fatty acids are supplied by vegetable oils, why butter? The question revolves around the issue of cholesterol and its adverse effects on the cardiovascular system. Naturally saturated fats (unhydrogenated) such as butter contain vitamin A and cholesterol. On the positive side, cholesterol is necessary for the production of vitamin D, hormones and bile salts.[3] It is also present in large quantity in the nerves and brain. In view of studies done on the effect of vitamin C and lecithin in preventing cholesterol deposits by keeping excess cholesterol in the bloodstream and circulating its way out of the body, it appears that a balanced intake of cholesterol and unsaturated fatty acids is beneficial to health when balanced by lecithin and vitamin C.[4]

If other sources of cholesterol are ingested daily, one may want to avoid the butter in these breakfast recipes entirely and increase the oil by a corresponding amount. The use of butter also introduces the problem of salt. For those desiring to avoid salt completely, unsalted or sweet butter should be used or all oil in place of the oil/butter com-

---

[1] Adelle Davis, *Let's Eat Right To Keep Fit,* pp. 42-49.

[2] See: Dr. Ruben, *The High Fiber Diet.*

[3] Adelle Davis, *Let's Eat Right To Keep Fit,* pp. 115-121.

[4] Linus Pauling, *Vitamin C The Common Cold and The Flu,* pp. 191-192.

bination. Iodine can then be supplied by the addition of kelp (up to 1 tsp. per batch of granola).

Every home should have its own brand of granola. Think of the tastes and textures you like best, and draw up a list of ingredients from them. What are your favorite nuts and seeds? How sweet do you like your cereal? Perhaps a bit of oil and no sweetener at all will suit your palate best. For a long lasting crunch, build your recipe around a core of cereal flakes. Brown rice flour and corn meal add a grainy crunch. Wheat, soy, triticale, oat and rye flours absorb moisture more readily than flakes and will clump if used exclusively, so add them in smaller amounts to vary the texture. Nuts and seeds alone can change the taste of a basic recipe. Peanuts do not taste at all like peanuts unless they have been roasted ahead of time and then added to the cereal as peanut butter, peanut meal or chopped peanuts. As a last word, lecithin should be an emulsifying agent for the nuts, butter and oil when ingested. Because of its high phosphorus content, it is recommended that lecithin granules be balanced with calcium and magnesium. Such balanced granules are readily available at health food and nutrition stores.

Stainless steel pans or cookie sheets should be used in baking because of all the turning involved in maintaining an evenly browned cereal. The granola should cover the entire sheet or pan to a depth of up to 1/2 inch. Do not crowd the pan, however, since this will make turning difficult. Bake the cereal at an oven temperature between 325 degrees F. and 350 degrees F. and check the trays at ten minute intervals. The edges will brown first, and it is necessary to lift the browned cereal with a metal spatula and move it to the center of the tray. The center portion should be gradually moved out toward the edges with each successive rotation of the cereal.

Baking time varies with ovens. Small ovens will brown the edges more quickly. Wood stoves tend to brown more evenly than electric. Gas stoves come closer to duplicating the effects of radiant wood heat. Whatever type of oven you have, be sure that the cereal is thoroughly dry when you remove it from the oven. This can be checked quickly by removing about one teaspoon of the cereal from the tray and allowing it to cool. Within a few minutes it will crisp if it is done cooking. There is no greater insult to the name of granola than sticky, not quite cooked oats. When the entire tray is golden, remove it from the oven, and let it cool completely on a wire or wooden rack before transferring the granola from the tray to storage containers. Use lidded glass or plastic jars for keeping. The lids should be tightly fastened to keep the cereal from absorbing moisture in the air and losing its crunch. Glass and plastic are recommended over tin cans or containers since oily grains, nuts and seeds tend to go rancid quicker in tins than in glass or plastic. Unless the granola will be eaten on a regular basis, and has been made in small batches, it is always a good idea to keep it refrigerated.

Branola

This granola is a taste and texture favorite for snacking and granola bars. It can be eaten straight or with raisins, or with milk. When spooned over a dish of yogurt and sliced bananas, it turns breakfast into dessert! These recipes for granola make a large quantity.

1/2 c. butter
1/2 c. cold pressed safflower oil
1 c. raw unfiltered honey
6 c. rolled oats
2 c. miller's bran
1 c. wheat germ
1 c. raw hulled sunflower seeds
1 c. raw coarsely chopped almonds
1 c. unsweetened grated coconut
1/4 c. raw unhulled sesame seeds
1/4 c. lecithin granules

1. Heat the butter, oil and honey over a low flame until liquefied.
2. In a large bowl combine the oats, bran, wheat germ, sunflower seeds, almonds, coconut, sesame seeds and lecithin.
3. Pour the honey/butter/oil mixture over the dry ingredients and stir until all the dry ingredients are thoroughly moistened. Stir up from the bottom of the bowl to be sure that the liquid mixture has evenly coated the oats and nuts.
4. Spread this mixture onto four ungreased cookie sheets (or two batches of two cookie sheets) and bake at 325-350 degrees F. for 30 minutes to 1 hour, depending upon the type of oven. Keep turning and rotating the cereal at intervals as the edges brown. When the granola has turned uniformly brown, remove the cookie sheets from the oven and let the cereal cool on the trays before removing for storage.

One cup of Branola provides approximately one-fourth to one-third the daily adult protein requirement, depending on individual weight.* A cup of milk will complement the seed protein and its additional 9 grams of protein will insure that you are getting the day off to a good start.

---

* One cup dry measure contains approximately 14 grams of total protein, based on the Protein Tables, pp. 99-114 in Lappe's *Diet for a Small Planet.*

Peanut Cashew Crunch

This cereal is lightly sweetened and packs more energy per serving than most granolas because of the addition of peanut butter. As in all recipes in this book, the cereal calls for home ground ingredients whenever possible, and the soy flour is no exception. Flour freshly ground from soybeans is known as "full-fat" soy, while most of the commercially available flours from soy are "de-fatted" and hence, more powdery. Either product may be used; flour made from the whole legume keeps the natural balance of nutrients intact, while de-fatted soy flour has almost three times the protein content of its unprocessed sister. Use a steel mill to grind soybeans.

Fresh bananas sliced over this cereal are a delicious taste complement and an excellent source of potassium.

1 c. homemade or "natural" creamy peanut butter
1 c. raw unfiltered honey
1/4 c. cold pressed safflower oil
1/4 c. butter
6 c. rolled oats
2 c. miller's bran
1/2 c. soy flour
1/2 c. wheat germ
1 c. powdered instant non-fat milk
1 c. chopped roasted peanuts
1 c. chopped raw cashews
1/4 c. lecithin granules
1 c. chopped pitted dates

1. In a saucepan warm over low heat until liquid the peanut butter, honey, oil and butter.
2. In a large bowl combine the oats, bran, soy flour, wheat germ, milk, peanuts, cashews and lecithin.
3. Pour the warmed liquid ingredients over the dry, mixing with a wooden spoon at first, then completing the mixing by hand if necessary until the peanut butter coating is evenly distributed over the cereal. The granola will be dry.
4. Bake on ungreased stainless cookie trays or pans at 325 degrees F. for 20 to 30 minutes or until evenly browned. Turn and rotate the cereal as the edges brown. Cool on the trays.

5. Stir in the dates. Depending on the consistency of the peanut butter you use, this cereal will usually retain its crunch even with the addition of dates to the cooked, cooled cereal. If you prefer, however, the dates may be sprinkled on the granola just before serving.

PEANUT BUTTER

Homemade peanut butter allows you to leave out the salt, which is usually added to commercially ground natural peanut butters. To make peanut butter, roast a thin layer of Spanish or Virginia peanuts, with skins, in a stainless pan at 325-350 degrees F. for 30 to 40 minutes. The peanuts will be lightly browned beneath their papers, and the heat will have brought the oil to the surface of the nuts. Be sure the nuts are roasted long enough. Cool one or two and taste them to check if their flavor meets your idea of what peanut butter should taste like. If they pass the palate test, cool the pan of peanuts; then grind in a Corona steel mill, blender or Salton peanut butter machine. If a blender is used, set it on shred or grind, add 1 to 1 1/2 cups roasted nuts and process. At first the resulting product will be the consistency of meal, but further processing will turn it into a flour.

Maple Pecan Granola

1/2 c. cold pressed safflower oil
1/2 c. butter
1 c. pure maple syrup
8 c. rolled oats
1 c. miller's bran
2 c. raw wheat germ
1 c. coarsely chopped or broken pecans (raw)
1 c. raw hulled sunflower seeds
1/4 c. lecithin granules

1. Over low heat melt the oil, butter and maple syrup.
2. In a large bowl, combine the oats, bran, wheat germ, pecans, sunflower seeds and lecithin.
3. Pour the liquid ingredients over the oat and seed mixture and stir with a wooden or stainless steel spoon until the dry ingredients are thoroughly and evenly moistened.
4. Spread the granola on ungreased stainless cookie sheets and bake at 350 degrees F. for 30 minutes or until evenly browned and crisp. Turn and rotate the cereal at 10 minute intervals, and check an oat flake occasionally to see if the cereal is done.
5. Cool the granola on the tray, then remove with a spatula and transfer to glass or plastic containers for storage.

Carob Granola

Brown rice flour gives this granola its unusual crunch. Commercially milled rice flours are often processed at high heat and the resulting product is extremely powdery. A hand operated steel mill or an electric stone mill will yield a grainier flour, with a texture ideally suited to granola.

The addition of milk powder to the carob and rice gives this cereal a malted milk taste.

1/2 c. cold pressed safflower oil
1/2 c. butter
1 c. raw unfiltered honey
1 c. brown rice flour
6 c. rolled oats
1 c. bran
1 c. raw wheat germ
2 c. powdered (instant) milk
2 c. coarsely chopped raw almonds
1 c. carob flour
1 c. unsweetened dried, shredded coconut
1/4 c. lecithin granules
1 tsp. cinnamon

1. Warm the oil, butter and honey until the butter is liquefied.
2. Combine in a large bowl the rice flour, oats, bran, wheat germ, milk, almonds, carob, coconut, lecithin and cinnamon.
3. Pour the liquid ingredients over the dry and stir thoroughly, until the honey/oil mixture is evenly distributed throughout the mix.
4. Spread the granola on stainless steel cookie trays and bake at 325 degrees F. for 20 minutes or until browned and crisp. This cereal must be watched carefully (at 5 minute intervals) because the milk powder and carob scorch easily. Turn and rotate the cereal frequently during baking.
5. Cool the granola on the trays; then remove with a spatula to storage containers.

Gingerbread Granola

This is a favorite snacking cereal. It needs no additional milk to complement its proteins and the distinctive taste is as habit forming as ginger snaps, if not more so!

Wheat and barley flour form small nuggets of crisp gingerbread when coated with the molasses/honey mix, and their protein is complemented by the sunflower seeds, milk and cashews. One-half cup of soy is an optional addition to the dry ingredients. It can be added in place of the powdered milk for those wishing to restrict milk intake while keeping protein levels high.

1/2 c. raw unfiltered honey
1/2 c. molasses
1/2 c. butter
1/2 c. cold pressed safflower oil
5 c. rolled oats
2 c. bran
1 c. wheat germ (raw)
1 c. hard red wheat flour (bread or graham flour)
1 c. barley flour
1 c. powdered instant non-fat milk
(1/2 c. soy flour—to sbtitute for milk powder)
1 c. raw hulled sunflower seeds
1 c. raw cashew pieces
1/4 c. lecithin granules
2 tsp. cinnamon
2 tsp. ginger

1. Warm until melted in a small saucepan the honey, molasses, butter and oil.
2. In a large bowl, measure and stir until combined the oats, bran, wheat germ, wheat and barley flours, milk or soy flour, sunflower seeds, cashews, lecithin, cinnamon and ginger.
3. Pour the warmed liquid ingredients over the dry mix and stir until it is thoroughly moistened.
4. Spread the granola on ungreased stainless cookie sheets and bake at 350 degrees F. for 30 minutes or until browned. Turn and rotate the cereal as the edges brown, usually at 10 minute intervals.
5. Cool on the trays before storing.
6. When serving, Thompson or Monukka raisins are a natural accompaniment to this cereal.

Sesame Cinnamon Crunch

2/3 c. raw unfiltered honey
1/3 c. cold pressed safflower oil
1/3 c. butter
1 tsp. cinnamon
5 c. rolled oats
1/2 c. soy flour
1 c. miller's bran
1 c. raw wheat germ
1 c. powdered instant non-fat milk
1 c. unsweetened dried grated coconut
1 c. raw hulled sunflower seeds
1 c. cashew pieces (raw)
1/2 c. raw unhulled sesame seeds
1/4 c. lecithin granules

1. In a small saucepan warm until melted the honey, oil, butter and cinnamon.
2. Measure into a large bowl and stir until combined the oats, soy flour, bran, wheat germ, milk, coconut, sunflower seeds, cashews, sesame seeds and lecithin.
3. Stir the liquid ingredients until the cinnamon is dispersed and pour the mixture over the dry ingredients, stirring until they are evenly moistened.
4. Spread the granola on ungreased stainless cookie trays and bake at 350 degrees F. for 30 minutes until browned and crisped. Turn and rotate several times during baking. Cool on the trays and then transfer to storage containers.

Cinnamon announces its presence meekly to some palates, while to others it comes on strong. If the full flavor of cinnamon is what you are seeking, increase the cinnamon in the honey/butter mixture to 2 tsp.

Banana Date Granola

The sweetening for this cereal comes mainly from the bananas and dates. Honey simply enhances the banana flavor.

Three bananas plus dates make this cereal a high potassium, high vitamin A breakfast.

Often recipes call for banana flakes instead of fresh whole bananas. Use caution in purchasing these flakes, for many have been sweetened with refined sugar, deep fried in highly saturated fats and artificially flavored.

Use bananas that are medium ripe; this means that the peels are well speckled with brown spots. Their flavor will be at its peak.

1/2 c. raw unfiltered honey
1/2 c. cold pressed safflower oil
1/4 c. butter
6 c. rolled oats
1 c. miller's bran
2 c. raw wheat germ
1 c. unsweetened dried shredded coconut
1 c. raw hulled sunflower seeds
1/2 c. chopped pitted dates
1/4 c. lecithin granules

1. Heat over low flame until melted the honey, oil and butter.
2. Measure into a large bowl and stir until combined the oats, bran, wheat germ, coconut, sunflower seeds, dates and lecithin.
3. Mash 3 medium sized bananas and set aside.
4. Pour the honey/oil mixture over the dry ingredients and stir thoroughly until the mix is evenly distributed. The granola will be dry at this point. Add the mashed bananas and stir thoroughly so that the banana is well blended into the cereal.
5. Spread the moist granola on ungreased stainless trays and bake at 350 degrees F. for 30 to 40 minutes, turning at 10 minute intervals until the moisture has evaporated and the cereal is crisp and golden. Cool on the trays before removing for storage.

Rollo Granola

This is a completely wheat free cereal, receiving its fiber from the greater proportion of cereal flakes and ground flax seed. Sunflower seeds keep the protein high, while molasses adds calcium, phosphorus, iron and potassium. Serve with raisins or chopped Black Mission figs, or a combination of both.

2 c. rolled rye (flakes)
6 c. rolled oats
1 c. coarsely chopped raw cashews
1 c. raw hulled sunflower seeds
1/2 c. flaxseed, ground*
1/4 c. lecithin granules
1 c. molasses
1/2 c. butter
1/2 c. cold pressed safflower oil

1. In a large bowl combine the rye flakes, oats, cashews, sunflower seeds, flaxseed and lecithin.
2. In a small saucepan, warm until liquid the molasses, butter and oil.
3. Pour the liquid ingredients over the dry and stir thoroughly until combined.
4. Transfer to 2 stainless cookie trays and bake at 350 degrees F. for 40 to 45 minutes, until lightly browned and crisp. Check the cereal at 10 minute intervals to turn and rotate.
5. Allow to cool on the trays before removing to lidded storage containers. Keep cool or refrigerate.

---

* The measure given for the ground flax is for the whole seed, which should then be ground coarsely in a Corona steel mill or blender. The grinding incorporates air, and the amount of ground flax will therefore be greater than 1/2 cup, but all should be used in the recipe.

Wheat Germ

Although rolled oats and other cereal flakes are the usual main components in crunchy granolas, they are by no means the last word in toasted breakfast cereals. Wheat germ is a cereal in its own right, with 12 grams of protein per half-cup serving. It is an excellent source of potassium and phosphorus, B1, B2 and niacin.

Fresh wheat germ is pale gold in color and smells delicious. Make sure that the wheat germ you serve meets both of these qualifications, since rancid wheat germ is disagreeable both to the taste buds and the digestive system. As a rich source of vitamin E and wheat germ oil, the flakes must be protected, through refrigeration, from oxidizing.

While wheat germ can be eaten raw, a light toasting improves the flavor without causing a serious loss of nutrients. Simply spread a thin layer of wheat germ in a stainless or enamelware pan and toast in the oven for 5-7 minutes at 275 degrees F. On top of the stove, in a dry cast iron skillet, the germ will take a little longer—10 to 15 minutes—over low heat with occasional stirring. The wheat germ can then be eaten with sliced fresh fruit, raisins, or fruit purees, such as applesauce or apricot puree. It can be sprinkled on yogurt or eaten as a regular cereal with any milk product.

Crunchy Wheat Germ is a special treat. For those who object to the taste of wheat germ, it's an ideal way to prepare this important food. The only drawback to eating straight wheat germ is the relatively low fiber content. Since fiber is extremely important in regulating body processes and protecting against environmental pollutants, wheat bran should be added if few or no other fiber sources are included in the diet.

Crunchy Wheat Germ

Enjoy this for breakfast or dessert. This recipe may be doubled, tripled or quadrupled.

1 T. cold pressed oil
1 T. raw unfiltered honey or pure maple syrup
(1/4 tsp. cinnamon)
1 c. raw wheat germ

1. Warm the oil, liquid sweetener and cinnamon in a pan.
2. Stir the liquid into the raw wheat germ and combine thoroughly with a wooden or stainless spoon. All the flakes should be uniformly coated.
3. Spread the moistened wheat germ on the bottom of an ungreased stainless or enamelware or glass pan and toast in a 350 degree F. oven for 20 minutes. Check after 10 minutes to see if the edges need to be turned in toward the center.
4. At the end of 20 minutes the wheat germ will still seem moist, but it will crisp upon cooling. When it is thoroughly cooled, transfer it to a tightly lidded container, glass or plastic, and refrigerate.

High Fiber Wheat Germ

This recipe can be doubled, tripled or quadrupled.

2 T. cold pressed safflower oil
2 T. honey (raw unfiltered)
1 1/2 c. raw wheat germ
1/2 c. miller's bran
(1/2 tsp. cinnamon)

1. In a small saucepan warm the oil and honey.
2. In a medium sized bowl, measure and mix the wheat germ, bran and cinnamon.
3. Stir the liquid ingredients into the wheat germ and bran, making sure to coat the dry ingredients uniformly.
4. Spread the high fiber wheat germ on the bottom of an ungreased stainless or enamelware pan and bake at 350 degrees F. for 20 minutes. Turn and rotate once, midway during baking.
5. Although the cereal will not appear to be done at the end of 20 minutes, remove it from the oven. It will crisp during cooling. Allow the cereal to cool in the pan and transfer to storage containers when room temperature. Refrigerate.

Wheat Germ Mixes

Regular Toasted, Crunchy Toasted, and High Fiber Wheat Germ can be combined with any of the following ingredients, depending upon individual preference and caloric allowances.

Seeds, raw or roasted (sunflower, pumpkin, chia, millet, sesame)
Roasted chopped peanuts
Chopped nuts, raw or roasted (pecans, almonds, cashews, walnuts, pine nuts, filberts, macadamias, pistachio, brazil, hickory)
Chopped dried fruits (dates, figs, raisins, pineapple, apricot, papaya, apple, banana)

The above ingredients can be added directly to the toasted wheat germ (plain, crunchy or high fiber) and stored in a closed container with the cereal. Fresh fruits can be added to the cereal bowl when the wheat germ is served.

Wheat germ mixes make a compact breakfast that is good when a light high protein cereal is desired. They can be eaten as a trail food or mixed with dairy or non-dairy milks and served in the conventional way. Layer the mix with yogurt or sprinkle it on top of the yogurt that's on top of the pancakes. Fold it inside crepes with a sauce.

The following two mixes are meant as suggestions only, to give you an idea of proportions when making up your own wheat germ mixes.

Crunchy Apricot Mix

1 c. Crunchy Wheat Germ or High Fiber Wheat Germ
1/2 c. chopped dried apricots
1/4 c. unsweetened shredded dried coconut
1/2 c. chopped raw cashews

1. Measure into a small bowl the Crunchy Wheat Germ or High Fiber Wheat Germ, apricots, coconut and cashews.
2. Stir and serve, or store in the refrigerator.

Crunchy Date Mix

1 c. Crunchy Wheat Germ or High Fiber Wheat Germ
1/2 c. chopped pitted dates
1/2 c. chopped raw almonds
1/4 c. toasted unhulled sesame seeds

1. Measure the following ingredients into a small bowl: the Crunchy Wheat Germ or High Fiber Wheat Germ, dates, almonds and sesame seeds.
2. Stir and serve, or store in the refrigerator.

Breakfast Bars

Travel, late sleeping habits, early trains, buses and car pools often make sitting down to the breakfast table a difficult goal to achieve. The joggers who get in a few miles before breakfast likewise find themselves short on time as they come into the home stretch.

For these people, breakfast bars are the answer. The purpose of breakfast bars is to combine high protein, high energy foods into portable servings that can be taken and eaten anywhere. Any granola can be made into a bar. Any combination of wheat germ cereals, seeds, nuts and fruits can also be made into a bar. The following recipes are but a sampler of endless possibilities.* Each of the following recipes makes one 8 x 8 square pan which can be cut into 15 bars.

---

* Wheat germ, nut and seed bars are the most concentrated sources of energy, since wheat germ provides approximately 12 grams of protein per half cup, plus a full complement of fatty acids, iron, calcium, phosphorus, potassium, B1, B2, niacin and fiber. Combined with high protein nuts and seeds it makes a convenient and compact bar for travellers and breakfasters on the run as well as for those who just prefer a bar to a bowl of cereal. Alone or especially when accompanied by a glass of milk or a bowl of yogurt, these bars are a sure way to get the day off to a great start.

The Commuter Special

Commuters are generally people who need bran. A hurried life and public transportation highlight the needs for adequate protein and fiber. Each bar provides approximately 6 1/2 grams of protein.

1 1/2 c. raw wheat germ
1 c. miller's bran
1 c. sesame seeds
1/2 c. raw chopped hulled sunflower seeds
1/2 c. chopped raisins or figs
1/2 c. raw unfiltered honey
3 T. butter or safflower oil

1. Measure into a stainless or enamelware 9 x 12 inch ungreased baking pan the wheat germ, bran and sesame seeds.
2. Toast these ingredients at 350 degrees F. for 20 minutes, checking occasionally to see if the edges need to be turned in toward the center.
3. Transfer to a medium sized mixing bowl and add the sunflower seeds and raisins or figs. Lightly oil an 8 x 8 inch pan and set aside.
4. Put the honey and oil in a small saucepan. Quickly bring these ingredients to a hard boil and continue to boil for 5 minutes, stirring constantly.
5. Immediately pour the hot mixture over the toasted ingredients and stir rapidly, making sure to distribute the honey/butter evenly throughout.
6. Spread the cereal into the oiled 8 x 8 inch pan and press it down flat, applying pressure with the back of a metal spatula or the palms of the hands. A light coating of oil on the spatula or hands will keep them from sticking.
7. Let the pan of cereal cool 5 to 10 minutes, then cut into 15 bars with a sharp knife. Let cool further, then remove, breaking the bars apart along the cut lines. Store and refrigerate in a lidded container.

Wrap pairs of bars in Saran wrap or plastic bags for convenience in packing into suitcases, backpacks, briefcases or pockets.

3-C Wheat Germ Bar

1 1/2 c. "plain" toasted wheat germ
3/4 c. finely chopped raw cashews
3/4 c. finely chopped raw almonds
1/3 c. unsweetened dried shredded coconut
1/3 c. raw chia seeds
1/2 c. honey (raw, unfiltered)
3 T. cold pressed safflower oil

1. In a medium bowl measure and combine the toasted wheat germ, cashews, almonds, coconut and chia seeds.
2. Place the honey and oil in a small saucepan and bring the mixture to a full rolling boil over medium heat. Boil hard for 5 minutes, stirring constantly to prevent scorching.
3. Pour the hot honey/oil mixture over the wheat germ and nut mix, stirring quickly and thoroughly. Make sure that all ingredients are coated. Immediately transfer the hot mixture into an oiled 8 x 8 pan.
4. With lightly oiled palms, press the mixture firmly into the bottom of the pan. Let cool 5 minutes and press down again. It is extremely important to compress the bar as much as possible or it will crumble. The recipe calls for only enough honey to bind the wheat germ, nuts and seeds when the ingredients are firmly pressed. Let cool another five minutes, then cut into 15 bars (3 cuts one way and 5 cuts the other).
5. When the bars are at room temperature, remove from the pan and wrap two together in clear plastic wrap or keep in a lidded container. Keep refrigerated.

Each bar contains approximately 5 grams of protein. Almonds are an excellent source of calcium, phosphorus and potassium and cashews are a good second in these three nutrients. Coconut boosts the potassium.

Sesame Apple Bars

1 1/2 c. "plain" toasted wheat germ
3/4 c. finely chopped dried apple
3/4 c. toasted unhulled sesame seeds*
3/4 c. finely chopped raw cashews
(1/4 tsp. cinnamon)
1/2 c. honey (raw, unfiltered)
3 T. cold pressed safflower oil

1. Into a medium sized bowl, measure and mix the wheat germ, apple, sesame seeds, cashews and cinnamon.
2. Place the honey and oil in a small saucepan. Bring to a full rolling boil and boil hard for 5 minutes, stirring constantly to prevent scorching.
3. Pour the hot liquid over the wheat germ mixture, taking care to scrape the saucepan with a rubber spatula to get out all of the honey/ oil. This recipe is designed for only enough sweetener to hold the ingredients together.
4. Stir quickly and thoroughly, then turn the warm mixture into an oiled 8 x 8 inch pan. Press down firmly with the back of a stainless spoon, metal spatula, or lightly oiled palms. Let cool for 5 minutes, then press again.
5. After 5 more minutes of cooling, slice with a sharp oiled knife into 15 bars. Watch to make sure that the entire pan does not set before you have cut it into bars, since it will harden more as it cools.
6. When the bars are room temperature, remove from the pan and wrap in clear plastic wrap, two per serving. Keep refrigerated.

Each bar contains approximately 6 grams of protein. The sesame seeds are an excellent source of calcium, phosphorus and potassium. Cashews provide the same three, plus vitamin A. The apples are high in potassium.

* Sesame seeds as well as wheat germ can be toasted in a dry cast iron skillet on top of the stove. Spread a 1/4 inch layer of wheat germ or sesame seeds in the bottom of the pan and set over low heat. Toast the wheat germ for 5-10 minutes, stirring every few minutes. The wheat germ will turn a slightly darker golden, but that is all. The sesame seeds will take between 10-20 minutes to toast thoroughly. Toasting brings out the full sesame seed flavor.

Carob Bars

1 1/2 c. lightly toasted plain wheat germ
3/4 c. chopped roasted peanuts, with skins
3/4 c. carob flour
1/3 c. powdered instant milk
1/2 c. honey
1 c. creamy natural peanut butter

1. Into a small bowl, measure and mix the toasted wheat germ, peanuts, carob and milk.
2. Place the honey in a medium sized saucepan. Over medium heat, bring the honey to a full rolling boil and boil for 5 minutes, stirring constantly to prevent scorching.
3. Add the peanut butter. Stir over low heat until the peanut butter is melted, and the mixture has the consistency of a cream sauce.
4. Add the dry ingredients to the peanut butter/honey and stir quickly and thoroughly. Turn the warm mixture into an oiled 8 x 8 inch pan and press down firmly. Cool for 5 minutes and press again.
5. Let cool an additional 5 minutes, then cut into 15 bars. When the bars are room temperature, wrap in 2 bar servings in clear plastic wrap. Refrigerate.

Each of these bars supplies approximately 10 grams of protein. Peanuts are a good source of calcium, phosphorus and potassium.

Peanut Apple Bars

Peanuts and sunflower seeds complement each other to provide over 7 grams of protein per bar.

1 1/2 c. "plain" toasted wheat germ
3/4 c. chopped roasted peanuts, with skins
3/4 c. chopped raw hulled sunflower seeds
3/4 c. finely chopped dried apple.
1/2 c. raw unfiltered honey
3 T. cold pressed safflower oil

1. In a medium sized bowl, combine the wheat germ, peanuts, sunflower seeds and apple.
2. Place the honey and oil in a small saucepan. Bring to a full rolling boil and boil for 5 minutes, stirring constantly to prevent scorching.
3. Pour the boiling liquid over the dry ingredients, stirring rapidly to distribute the honey/oil evenly over the wheat germ and nuts.
4. Transfer the mixture to a lightly oiled 8 x 8 inch pan and press down firmly with the back of a stainless spoon or spatula. Cool for 5 minutes and press again with lightly oiled palms, compacting the bars as much as possible.
5. Let cool an additional 5 minutes, then cut into 15 bars. When the bars are cool, wrap in 2 bar servings in clear plastic wrap or in a tightly lidded container and refrigerate.

Granola Squares

Granola squares can be taken anywhere and eaten anywhere, without bowls or spoons. Made basically from cereal flakes, wheat germ, nuts, fruits and seeds, they are a bit bulkier than wheat germ bars per gram of protein, but they pack more fiber. All cereal flakes preserve the bran layer of the whole berry and additional wheat bran insures the proper movement of food through the digestive system as well as protection against pollutants. Persons allergic to wheat can substitute more rolled oats, rolled rye, nuts or seeds for the high fiber (bran) component of wheat; and soy, peanuts or seeds for the high protein (germ) component of wheat.

A boiled syrup of honey, molasses, maple syrup, sorghum, or a combination of these does the best job of holding the dry ingredients together. For this reason, the flakes, nuts and seeds should be toasted without any liquid coating as they are for regular granola. This can be done by measuring the dry ingredients into a 9 x 12 inch stainless or enamelware pan and baking them at 350 degrees F. for 20-30 minutes. Wheat germ should be added to the pan for the last 10 minutes of toasting only. The grains and seeds should be checked occasionally and turned if the edges begin to brown.

While the dry ingredients are cooling, the syrup should be brought to a boil. It is not necessary to cool the dry component any longer than it takes to make the syrup, which should be poured over the dry ingredients immediately and stirred vigorously. It is essential to mix up these squares rapidly and transfer them to an oiled 8 x 8 inch pan before the syrup hardens.

The proportion of syrup to flakes and other additions varies slightly from that for regular granola. **Approximately 4 cups of dry ingredients require 3/4 cup syrup.** Favorite granola recipes (unsweetened) can be mixed up, toasted plain, then turned into squares according to these proportions. Liquid lecithin combines best with the syrup. Safflower oil is recommended, but any cold pressed vegetable oil may be used. Butter may substitute for up to half of the oil requirement.

As in all breakfast recipes, the ingredients are balanced for maximum protein, fiber, fatty acids, vitamins, minerals and good taste. A glass of milk or side dish of yogurt add complimentary proteins.

Batch recipes are geared for two persons (1 - 8 x 8 pan), but can easily be doubled and put into a 9 x 12 pan for larger families.

Coconut Squares

Two squares provide approximately 12 g. of protein. Since coconut is relatively low in protein, the proportion of wheat germ has been increased.

> 2 c. rolled oats
> 1/2 c. unsweetened dried shredded coconut
> 1/4 c. raw hulled sunflower seeds
> 1/4 c. chopped raw almonds
> 1/4 c. miller's bran
> 3/4 c. raw wheat germ
> 1/2 c. raw unfiltered honey
> 3 T. butter or safflower oil
> 1 T. liquid lecithin

1. Measure the oats, coconut, sunflower seeds, almonds and bran into a 9 x 12 inch baking pan and toast at 350 degrees F. for 20 minutes.
2. Add the wheat germ and toast for an additional 10 minutes. Transfer the above ingredients to a medium sized bowl.
3. Place the honey, oil and liquid lecithin in a small saucepan. Bring to a boil then reduce the heat and boil hard for 5 minutes, stirring to prevent scorching.
4. Pour the hot honey/oil over the dry ingredients. (1/4 tsp. vanilla may be added at this point.) Stir quickly and thoroughly to make sure that all ingredients are coated.
5. Transfer the hot mixed cereal to a lightly oiled 8 x 8 inch pan. Let cool 1-2 minutes, then press down firmly with oiled palms.
6. When the cereal is room temperature, cut with a serrated knife into 9 squares. Transfer to a storage container or wrap in clear plastic wrap and refrigerate.

Maple Squares

Two squares provide 13 grams of protein.

2 c. rolled oats
1/2 c. chopped raw cashews
1/4 c. raw hulled sunflower seeds
1/4 c. chopped raw pecans
1/4 c. miller's bran
1/2 c. raw wheat germ
2 T. honey
1/2 c. minus 2 T. pure maple syrup
2 T. cold pressed safflower oil
1 T. butter
1 T. liquid lecithin
1/4 tsp. vanilla

1. Measure the oats, cashews, sunflower seeds, pecans and bran into a stainless or enamelware pan (9 x 12 inch) and bake for 20 minutes at 350 degrees F.
2. Add the wheat germ and toast an additional 10 minutes. Transfer these ingredients to a medium sized bowl and prepare the syrup.
3. Spoon the honey into a half-cup measure. Fill to the top with maple syrup. Pour the honey/maple syrup into a small saucepan. Add safflower oil, butter and lecithin.
4. Bring the liquids to a full rolling boil, reduce heat and boil for 10 minutes, stirring occasionally to keep the syrup from scorching. Just before pouring over dry ingredients, add the vanilla.
5. Pour the boiling syrup over the dry toasted ingredients and stir rapidly to coat the oats and nuts thoroughly.
6. Transfer the coated mix into a lightly oiled 8 x 8 inch pan. Let cool 1-2 minutes, then press firmly with oiled palms. When the pan is room temperature, cut it into 9 squares.
7. Wrap the squares in clear plastic wrap or store in a tightly lidded glass or plastic container and refrigerate.

☀ Cinnamon Apple Squares

Two squares provide approximately 16 1/2 grams of protein.
High fiber sesame seeds take the place of additional bran in this recipe.

2 1/2 c. rolled oats
1/2 c. raw unhulled sesame seeds
1/3 c. wheat germ
1/2 c. raw hulled sunflower seeds
1/2 c. chopped dried apple
1/2 tsp. cinnamon
1/2 c. raw unfiltered honey
3 T. butter or oil
1 T. liquid lecithin

1. Toast the oats and sesame seeds in an ungreased 9 x 12 inch pan for 20 minutes at 350 degrees F.
2. Add the wheat germ and toast for an additional 10 minutes.
3. While these ingredients are toasting, place the dried apple into a medium sized bowl. Add the toasted ingredients plus the cinnamon and stir until well mixed.
4. Prepare the syrup by placing into a small saucepan the honey, oil or butter and lecithin. Bring the liquid ingredients to a full boil over medium heat; reduce heat and keep at a full boil for 5 minutes, stirring to avoid scorching. Pour the liquid over the dry ingredients, stirring rapidly to coat the oats/seeds, apple mixture evenly. Transfer to a lightly oiled 8 x 8 inch pan and let cool 1 to 2 minutes. Then press down firmly into the bottom of the pan.
6. When the mixture is room temperature, and it has hardened, cut it into 9 bars (3 cuts in each direction). Store in a lidded container or individually wrapped portions. Refrigerate.

Molasses Squares

Rye and molasses give these squares a distinctive flavor. Flax takes the place of bran, providing high fiber, and sunflower seeds substitute for wheat germ as sources of concentrated protein, making these an excellent breakfast bar for the wheat allergic.

Each square provides approximately 7 grams of protein.

2 c. rolled oats
1 c. rolled rye
1/4 c. flax seed, ground
1/2 c. raw hulled sunflower seeds
1/3 c. raisins, chopped figs or dates
2 T. honey
molasses (1/2 c. minus 2 T.)
3 T. butter or cold pressed oil
1 T. liquid lecithin

1. In a 9 x 12 inch pan measure the oats, rye, flax seed and sunflower seeds. Mix and bake for 30 minutes.
2. Transfer to a medium bowl and add the raisins, figs or dates.
3. Prepare syrup by measuring the honey into a 1/2 c. measure. Fill to the top with molasses. Pour the molasses/honey into a small saucepan along with the butter or oil and lecithin. Bring the molasses/oil mixture to a full rolling boil. Reduce heat and simmer, at a gentle boil, for 10 minutes.
4. Pour the boiling liquid over the toasted ingredients and stir vigorously to coat all grains and seeds evenly. Transfer the hot mixture to a lightly oiled 8 x 8 inch glass, stainless or enamelware pan.
5. Let cool 1-2 minutes, then press firmly with the back of a spoon or lightly oiled palms. Cool to room temperature. Then cut into 9 squares. Store in a lidded container, or covered, in the refrigerator.

Branola Sandwich Squares

1 1/2 c. rolled oats
1/2 c. miller's bran
1/2 c. raw hulled sunflower seeds
1/2 c. chopped raw almonds
1/2 c. unsweetened dried grated coconut
2 T. raw unhulled sesame seeds
1/2 c. raw wheat germ
1/2 c. honey
3 T. butter or oil
1 T. liquid lecithin

1. In a 9 x 12 inch baking pan, measure and mix the oats, bran, sunflower seeds, almonds, coconut and sesame seeds. Bake at 350 degrees F. for 20 minutes.
2. Add the wheat germ and bake an additional 10 minutes. Transfer the toasted ingredients to a medium sized bowl.
3. Prepare the "sandwich" filling (recipes follow below).
4. Measure the honey, butter or oil and lecithin into a small saucepan and bring to a boil. Simmer, boiling gently, for 10 minutes.
5. Pour over the toasted ingredients and stir until the honey/butter has coated the branola mix.
5. Transfer half the coated cereal to a lightly oiled 8 x 8 inch pan. Distribute the branola evenly over the bottom of the pan and press firmly with a metal spatula or oiled hands. Crumble the filling (recipe follow below) over the entire pan, then cover with the remaining half of the branola. Again press as firmly as possible. (It helps to have the fillings prepared ahead of time and chilled, since the hot branola mix will cause them to melt temporarily, although they will firm up again upon cooling.)
6. Cool to room temperature. Cut into 16 squares, and refrigerate, either in the pan, covered, or wrapped in individual portions.

Carob Filling

> 1/2 c. carob flour
> 1/2 c. powdered instant non-fat milk
> 1/4 c. roasted soy flour, see below
> 2 T. pure maple syrup
> 2 T. cold pressed safflower oil
> 1 T. liquid lecithin

1. Combine the carob, milk and soy flour.
2. Add the syrup, oil and lecithin. Mix until blended. The mixture will be dry. Add 1-2 T. water, just enough to make the filling bind. Work briefly with the fingertips, then gather up into a ball and chill before using, or simply crumble the carob from the ball onto the bottom layer of the branola sandwich..

Peanut Butter Filling
   Peanuts and milk step up the protein level of these breakfast sandwiches.

> 3/4 c. creamy "natural" or homemade peanut butter
>   (See page 33.)
> 1/2 c. powdered instant non-fat milk
> 1-2 T. honey, to taste

1. In a small bowl combine the peanut butter, milk and honey.
2. Mix these ingredients thoroughly and gather into a ball. Chill. The mixture firms up upon chilling and is then easier to distribute over the bottom layer of the branola sandwich. However, it can be used immediately and will firm as the sandwiches cool.

ROASTED SOY FLOUR ─────────────────
   Small amounts of soy flour (ground either by hand in a Corona mill, in the blender, in a Marathon Uni-Mill, or purchased pre-ground) are most easily roasted on top of the stove in a dry skillet. Cast iron, since it is heavy and distributes heat evenly, works best. Simply spread a 1/4 inch layer of soy flour in the bottom of the pan and roast over low heat until the flour begins to brown lightly, usually 5-10 minutes. Stir frequently to achieve a uniform roasting.

Puffed Cereals

When puffed commercially, wheat, corn, rice and millet literally explode. However, the nutritional value of these cereals based on a protein content to volume ratio is low. It takes over 7 cups of plain puffed wheat, for example, to equal 10 grams of protein. This makes puffed cereals a popular commercial item; a small quantity of cereal, when popped or puffed, will fill a large box. Now for the good news. You can feel good about serving puffed cereals to the family. By adding wheat germ and protein complementing nuts or seeds to plain puffed cereals (unsweetened), you can turn all that volume into something of substance.

Honey Puffed Wheat Cereal

There are 10 grams of protein in a 1 1/2 c. serving of honey puffed wheat cereal.

1/4 c. raw unfiltered honey
3 T. cold pressed safflower oil
1 T. butter
4 c. puffed wheat
1/4 c. raw unhulled sesame seeds
1 c. raw wheat germ
1 T. lecithin granules

1. Warm the honey, oil and butter in a saucepan until liquid.
2. Measure and combine in a medium bowl the wheat, sesame seeds, wheat germ and lecithin.
3. Pour the liquid ingredients over the dry and stir thoroughly so that all of the puffed wheat is coated with the honey mixture.
4. Spread the cereal on a stainless cookie tray (unoiled) and bake for 20 to 30 minutes at 325 degrees F. Check the cereal after the first 10 minutes, then every 5 minutes thereafter. Rotate the cereal as the edges brown. It is done when the puffed wheat is golden.
5. Let cool on the tray then transfer to storage containers and keep cool.

Puffed Coconut Rice Cereal

4 c. puffed rice
1 c. raw wheat germ
1/4 c. dried shredded coconut
1/4 c. ground almonds
1/4 c. raw unfiltered honey
3 T. cold pressed safflower oil
1 T. butter

1. Measure and mix in a medium bowl the puffed rice, wheat germ, coconut and almonds.
2. Warm the honey, oil and butter in a saucepan until liquid.
3. Pour the warmed liquid ingredients over the rice mixture and stir until all the ingredients are coated with the honey/oil.
4. Spread the cereal on a stainless cookie sheet and bake at 325 degrees F. for 20 to 30 minutes. Check after 10 minutes and rotate the cereal as the edges brown.
5. When uniformly golden in color, remove from the oven, let cool on the tray and then transfer to storage containers. Refrigerate.

Pancakes

Flat and Stack

Pancakes come in all shapes, sizes and textures. For some, they are a prerequisite of morning, for others, they are a Saturday morning treat. Well I remember my husband shaping rabbits and snowmen from pancake batter for his children's plates. Then the refined flour disappeared from our home, and the griddle became an ornament instead of a utensil for use.

Whole wheat pancakes are hardly formidable, however, and it is only a step further to a wide variety of whole grain hotcakes and crepes. In fact, the combinations of different flours, protein boosting additions, sauces and fillings are so extensive that the list of pancake recipes could quickly become astronomical. For this reason, this chapter, like those preceding it, is only an introduction to the world of pancakes. There are five basic types of pancakes: 1) flat, 2) stack, 3) oven pancakes, 4) blender pancakes and 5) yeast. Flat pancakes come in two types, the classic crepe and the Swedish. The crepe relies heavily on egg to make it tender and elastic, while milk is used to thin the batter of the somewhat thicker Swedish pancake.

A word on eggs is in order to those who are fearful of cholesterol. Eggs provide an almost perfect protein, 96% of which is readily assimilated by the digestive system. There is no danger of cholesterol build-up caused solely by eating eggs, since the yolk, a rich source of cholesterol, is equally rich in lecithin, which homogenizes fats and cholesterol. The lecithin keeps the fatty particles suspended and moving in the blood stream, thus preventing deposits on the artery walls.[1]

Neither the crepe nor Swedish pancake calls for baking powder, which gives the stack pancake its characteristic rise. Stack pancakes are literally small round cakes baked in a frying pan or griddle. Their texture closely resembles that of oven baked cakes. In most recipes for stack pancakes, the cook has the option of separating the eggs or blending them whole. The incorporation of stiffly beaten egg whites makes for a thicker batter and hence, a higher pancake. Wheat cakes, especially, benefit from the separation, but some of the other grains, such as oat and triticale, do not have the gluten to hold the rise and hence fare better when the whole eggs are beaten into the batter. The time involved in preparation is basically the same whether one chooses to separate the eggs or beat them in whole. Batters that incorporate the whole beaten egg need to stand at least 15 to 20 minutes, actually longer than the time it takes to separate the eggs and

[1] Adelle Davis, *Let's Eat Right To Keep Fit,* pp. 47, 118.

beat the whites. Batters that fold in the beaten egg whites can be baked on the griddle immediately.

Oven pancakes are exactly that–batters baked in the oven. They require more time–up to an hour's cooking time–but offer the bonus of looking after themselves while the cook is busy preparing lunches, jogging, practicing yoga or whatever.

Blender pancakes vary in thickness and are so categorized because whole soaked grains are whipped up into freshly ground batters. They are a novel approach to whole grain cooking and insure that the cereals are at their freshest. Blenders also enable the cook to create nut cakes and crepes that would otherwise be out of reach. There is no reason why a blender could not also be used for making other pancake batters with whole eggs, but the blender is not necessary. Consequently, only those recipes that require a blender are included here.

Finally, there are the yeast pancakes, some of which call for starting the batter the night before, others only fifteen minutes ahead of time. Yeast pancakes have a rise like stack pancakes. Nutritionally they are superior. Minerals such as zinc, iron and calcium can be bound up in the intestine by phytic acid, which is present in the bran layer of cereal grains; while the body produces an enzyme, phytase, to break down the salts formed by phytic acid and minerals, whole wheat and rye also contain this enzyme, which is released in the warm, moist conditions of dough rising. Yeasted pancakes, then, optimize the nutrients in the whole grains, while adding the extra protein of the yeast itself.

Pancakes are a boon to the wheat allergic or milk allergic, since no one ingredient is vital. If wheat is definitely restricted from one's diet, crepes, yeast and blender pancakes can provide a tantalizing array of alternatives. If it's milk that is causing problems, try substituting fruit juices, soy milk, or sesame, almond and cashew milks. There are even eggless pancakes, such as yeasted buckwheat.

While syrups are the traditional companions of pancakes, see what fruit sauces can do to turn the old standbys into tempting treats. Fresh fruit, cubed, mashed or sliced, and yogurt make a great topping for any category of cakes. Fill the crepes with cheese and nuts or peanut butter spread, then drizzle with syrup or spoon on the fruit sauce. Pure maple syrup and butter are only a beginning. Vary the family's favorites by sprinkling sesame seeds on the griddle or crepe pan. Seeds not only complement and increase the protein, but add fiber and a surprisingly delicious crunch.

Stack Pancakes

These are the traditional rounded cakes. Every natural foods kitchen has the ingredients necessary to make nutritious pancakes that are a delight to eat. Almost any grain, nut, legume or seed can be turned into a pancake, so don't hesitate to incorporate your favorite flavors in any recipe.

The only absolute in making stack cakes is the griddle. It has to be of heavy guage metal, preferably cast iron, but a well seasoned cast aluminum griddle will work. Cast iron transfers important trace iron to the pancakes, yielding a nutritionally superior product. If the griddle is new, season it by heating then coating with a thin layer of good quality oil (cold pressed safflower or corn). Allow the griddle to cool. The griddle may also be preheated in an oven, coated with safflower oil, and then allowed to cool down with the oven. When using a griddle for the first time after seasoning, spread a thin layer of cooking oil over the surface after heating and just before pouring or spooning on the batter. For completely oil free frying, a soapstone griddle is the answer. These never require oil of any kind. They are self-seasoning, absorbing the oil in the batter over a period of time. Their evenly distributed heat produces perfect, golden pancakes with a classic rise. Whichever griddle is used, however, there is a definite method to making well "crowned" pancakes. Hold the ladle or spoon containing the batter close to the griddle and let the batter flow out from the center of the mound. Dropping the batter from a height of even a few inches will result in an uneven cake.

Buttermilk can be substituted in any recipe for skim milk solids. Simply adjust the recipe: replace 1 1/2 tsp. baking powder with 1/2 tsp. baking soda. In all recipes, the baking powder called for is Rumford's or its equivalent, which contains no sodium aluminum sulfate. It relies upon calcium acid phosphate and bicarbonate of soda for leavening action. Baking powder can be prepared fresh at home by mixing two parts of cream of tartar with one part bicarbonate of soda.

However, never mix more than is needed, since the mixture does not store well.

The pilot recipes for stack pancakes are Wheat Griddlecakes and Soft Wheat Cakes (Fruited/Unfruited). Most of the other recipes are variations and adaptations of these two. Any flour, except corn and brown rice, can be substituted for wheat flour. Other grains, such as oat, rye, triticale, barley and buckwheat more closely resemble pastry wheat flour in the amount of moisture they absorb, so always make sure the total amount of flour and/or nutritional boosters equals 1 cup. Pancakes made 100% from these grains should then follow the recipe for Soft Wheat Cakes. For mixed grains, such as Buckwheat/ Rye, Wheat/Oat, Barley/Oat, Barley/Wheat, you should use proportions totalling one cup. Try 3 or 4 grain flours, a third or fourth cup of each, always totalling 1 cup of flour for each batch. For example, Soy/Wheat Cakes can be turned into Soy/Oat cakes or Soy/Buckwheat cakes by measuring 1/4 cup soy flour into a one cup measure and filling level with oat or buckwheat flour, then proceding as for Soy/Wheat cakes. Likewise, Carob/Oat cakes are simply a matter of substituting 3/4 cup oat flour for 3/4 cup pastry flour in the Carob Cake Recipe.

Corn and rice, when milled at home, are grainy and require a few minutes of soaking to make a smooth textured pancake. Rolled grains, such as barley, wheat, rye and triticale, benefit from the same method.

Wheat Griddlecakes

Hard wheat flour absorbs more moisture than soft white wheat or pastry wheat. Generally, 7/8 cup of hard wheat is the baking equivalent of 1 cup of pastry wheat. In converting favorite refined flour recipes to whole grain versions, bear in mind that the amount of flour must be reduced if hard wheat is used. Pastry wheat can usually be substituted cup for cup of refined flour.

When substituting nutritional boosters, such as soy or wheat germ, or other flours in place of hard wheat flour, measure the boosters into a one cup measuring cup and then fill to a level cupful of hard wheat flour instead of 7/8 cup. The reason for this is that other ingredients do not absorb moisture in the same quantity as hard wheat and the batter will be too thin if the total ingredients only measure 7/8 cup. Hard wheat flour alone, however, makes the best stack cake in the ratio of 7/8 cup flour to 1 cup milk.

This classic cake should be first served with butter and pure maple syrup. Then branch out and try adding a dollop of yogurt to the stack and a ladle of fruit sauce. One half cup of yogurt adds 6 grams of complementary protein.

7/8 c. hard wheat flour
1/4 tsp. sea salt or powdered kelp
1 1/2 tsp. baking powder
1 tsp. lecithin granules
2 eggs
1/3 c. powdered instant non-fat milk
1 c. water
2 1/2 T. cold pressed safflower oil
1 tsp. honey

1. In a medium bowl, measure and combine the flour, salt or kelp, baking powder and lecithin.
2. Into two small bowls, separate the eggs.
3. To the yolks, add the milk, water, oil and honey and whisk until blended.
4. Pour the liquid ingredients into the dry, whisking until smooth. Let this batter sit for 10 minutes.
5. During this time, beat the 2 egg whites until they form stiff peaks.
6. Heat the griddle.

7. Pour a small amount of the batter into the beaten whites, folding thoroughly with a rubber spatula. When this mixture is smooth and homogeneous, gradually fold it into the rest of the batter (in the medium sized bowl).

8. Ladle or spoon the batter onto a hot giddle, oiled or well-seasoned, holding the ladle close to the griddle. Bake until the tops bubble and the undersides are brown, about 2-3 minutes. The edges will be dry. Turn and bake for an additional 1-2 minutes.

9. Serve immediately in stacks of 3 or in a row of overlapping cakes.

Each serving of five or six 4 inch pancakes contains 19 grams of protein.

Soft Wheat Cakes
(Fruited/Unfruited)

This is the recipe to use for blueberry pancakes, lingonberry, chopped cranberry or apple cakes, or almost any fruit pancake. The tender crumb and delicate flavor of pastry wheat flour make these rounds of wheat and fruit truly "pan cakes." Even without the fruit, Soft Wheat Cakes are bound to become a favorite whole grain pancake.

  1 c. pastry wheat flour
  1/4 tsp. sea salt or powdered kelp
  1 1/2 tsp. baking powder
  1 tsp. lecithin granules
  2 eggs
  1/3 c. powdered instant non-fat milk
  1 c. water
  2 1/2 T. cold pressed safflower oil
  1 tsp. honey (raw, unfiltered)

1. In a medium bowl, measure and combine the flour, salt or kelp, baking powder and lecithin.
2. Into 2 small bowls, separate the eggs.
3. Add the milk, water, oil and honey to the yolks.
4. Combine the liquid and dry ingredients with a whisk, stirring until smooth. Let stand.
5. Beat the egg whites until they form stiff peaks.
6. Heat the griddle.
7. Fold a small amount of the batter (about 1/4 cup) into the beaten egg whites until smooth. Then fold this mixture into the batter.

Unfruited Cakes

Bake on the griddle as for Wheat Griddlecakes, page 66.

Fruited Cakes

If using fresh blueberries, chopped apple or any other fresh fruit, fold in 1 cup fruit as the final addition to the batter before baking. If using frozen blueberries or cranberries, ladle the batter onto the hot oiled griddle first, then sprinkle the berries on top of each cake. Since freezing bursts the cell walls, frozen berries will turn the batter blue. By adding the frozen berries to the pancake as it begins to set on the griddle, the cake retains its golden color and the blueberries hold their juice.

When the tops bubble and sides are dry (2-3 minutes), turn the cakes and bake an additional 1-2 minutes, until golden. Thick pancakes can always be tested as for cake, by inserting a clean toothpick in the center. If it comes out clean, the pancake is done.

Buck Wheat Cakes

Use home ground buckwheat for a high fiber, high protein treat. Buckwheat flavor is strong—a quarter cup goes a long way toward evoking childhood memories of lumberjack stacks.

The buckwheat flour can be raw or roasted. Measure 1/4 cup finely ground buckwheat flour in the bottom of a 1 cup measure. Fill to 1 cup level with hard wheat flour and proceed with instructions for Wheat Griddlecakes. See page 66. Omit or add fruit, as desired.

ROASTED BUCKWHEAT FLOUR

For the "Aunt Jemimah" flavor, pre-roast the buckwheat groats (as for peanuts, page 15) before grinding or pan roast the flour (as for soy flour, page 57).

Wheat Soy Cakes

One serving of these pancakes provides 21 g. of protein, even before the complement of yogurt or a glass of milk!

Measure 1/4 cup full fat soy flour in the bottom of a one cup measure. Fill to 1 cup level with hard wheat flour. Follow instructions for Wheat Griddlecakes, page 66.

Carob Cakes

Like brownies, these pancakes are irresistible. They satisfy the sweet tooth without the addition of sugar. Try them on diehard chocolate fans.

3/4 c. whole wheat pastry flour
1/4 c. carob flour
1/4 tsp. sea salt or powdered kelp
1/4 tsp. cinnamon
1 tsp. lecithin granules
1 1/2 tsp. baking powder
2 eggs
1 T. pure maple syrup
1/3 c. powdered instant non-fat milk
1 c. water
2 1/2 T. cold pressed safflower oil

1. In a medium sized bowl, combine the flour, carob, salt or kelp, cinnamon, lecithin and baking powder.
2. Into 2 small bowls, separate the eggs.
3. Add to the yolks, whisking until blended, the maple syrup, milk, water and oil.
4. Combine and bake as for Wheat Griddlecakes, page 66.

Wheat Rye Griddlecakes

1/2 c. hard wheat flour
1/2 c. whole rye flour
1/4 tsp. sea salt or powdered kelp
1 tsp. lecithin granules
2 eggs
1/3 c. powdered instant non-fat milk
1 c. water
2 1/2 T. cold pressed safflower oil
1 T. molasses or maple syrup

1. In a medium bowl, measure and combine the wheat flour, rye flour, salt or kelp, and lecithin.
2. Into 2 small bowls, separate the eggs.
3. Add to the yolks the milk, water, oil and sweetener.
4. Pour the liquid ingredients into the dry, whisking until smooth. Let stand.
5. Beat the egg whites to stiff peaks.
6. Heat the griddle.
7. Fold a small amount of the batter into the egg whites, and when thoroughly combined, fold this mixture into the rest of the batter.
8. Bake on a hot seasoned griddle or soapstone for 2-3 minutes, turning when the tops are bubbled and the sides are dry. Bake an additional 1-2 minutes, until the undersides are golden.
9. Serve with pure maple syrup and yogurt or with a raisin, fig or date sauce.

Buckwheat Oat Cakes

These are completely wheat free and delightfully light. High protein oat and buckwheat flours combine to surpass the protein content of regular wheat cakes. 100% buckwheat flour, ground from sprouting buckwheat tends to produce a tough pancake because of the dark husk coat. Ground buckwheat groats, which have the husk removed, would yield a finer pancake and could be used for the total amount of flour in this recipe. The incorporation of oat flour, however, gives this pancake a more tender crumb.

Measure into a medium bowl 2/3 c. buckwheat flour and 1/3 c. oat flour. Proceed as for Wheat Griddlecakes, page 66, using these ingredients in place of hard wheat flour.

Any pancake can be turned into a wheat germ cake by measuring 3 T. wheat germ into the bottom of the measuring cup used to measure the flour, then filling the cup to the required level with any flour—hard wheat, soft wheat, oat, rye, triticale, barley or buckwheat.

If you substitute more than 3 T. (up to 1/4 c.) of wheat germ for flour, or if you use 100% oat or triticale flour, be sure to beat the eggs *whole.* All batters calling for whole beaten eggs improve upon standing at least 15-20 minutes. This is not necessary when the eggs are separated.

Wheat Germ Oat Cakes

In terms of protein, oats are low calorie when compared to an equal quantity of wheat. Oat flour can be ground at home in a variety of ways. The freshest flour will be obtained by grinding whole oat groats in a steel or stone mill. However, oat flour can also be obtained by grinding rolled oats in the blender until a fine powder is produced.

Oat flour produces a thinner, sweeter pancake than wheat flour, so be ready to stack them high!

Try sprinkling raw unhulled sesame seeds on the hot griddle before ladling on the pancake batter to enhance the flavor and protein content of these cakes.

2/3 c. oat flour
1/3 c. wheat germ
1/4 tsp. sea salt or powdered kelp
1 1/2 tsp. baking powder
1 tsp. lecithin granules
2 whole eggs
2 T. cold pressed safflower oil
1 tsp. raw unfiltered honey
1 c. water
1/3 c. powdered instant non-fat milk

1. Measure into a medium bowl the oat flour, wheat germ, salt or kelp, baking powder and lecithin.
2. In a small bowl beat together the eggs, oil, honey, water and milk.
3. Pour the liquid ingredients into the dry and combine rapidly with a wire whisk. Let the batter stand for 15-20 minutes.
4. Heat the griddle during this time.
5. Ladle the batter onto the hot, seasoned griddle and let cook until the tops are bubbly and the bottoms are browned, about 2-3 minutes. Turn and bake an additional 1-2 minutes, until the undersides are evenly browned.

Stir the batter frequently while pouring onto the griddle, since the batter will separate upon standing.

Wheat Germ Sesame Cakes

Substitute 2/3 c. whole wheat pastry flour for oat flour in the Wheat Germ/Oat recipe. Sprinkle raw unhulled sesame seeds on the griddle and the tops of the pancakes before turning.

Triticale Cakes

When triticale flour is used in pancakes, like oat flour, it works best when the eggs are not separated, but beaten whole. It, too, produces a thinner, lighter flavored pancake and goes well with sesame seeds sprinkled on the griddle. The whole triticale berry, a cross breed of rye and wheat, can be ground the same as any whole grain in a steel or stone mill.

1 c. whole ground triticale flour
1/4 tsp. sea salt or powdered kelp
1 1/2 tsp. baking powder
1 tsp. lecithin granules
2 whole eggs
1 c. water
1 tsp. honey
1/3 c. powdered instant non-fat milk
2 T. cold pressed safflower oil

1. In a medium bowl, measure and combine the triticale flour, sea salt or kelp, baking powder and lecithin.
2. Into a small bowl, beat together the eggs, water, honey, milk and oil.
3. Combine liquid ingredients with dry. Let stand while heating the griddle, about 15-20 minutes.
4. Ladle onto the hot seasoned griddle and bake 2-3 minutes, until the tops are well bubbled and the sides are beginning to dry. Then turn and cook an additional 1-2 minutes, until the undersides are evenly browned.
5. Serve with butter, maple syrup or fruit sauce, and yogurt.

Wheatnut Cakes

Wheat plus milk plus peanuts make these cakes a triple protein breakfast. For peanut butter fans, they are a must. Pastry flour allows the peanuts to dominate, while hard wheat flour results in a more subtle blend of flavors.

1 c. whole wheat pastry flour
   OR 7/8 c. hard wheat flour
1/4 tsp. sea salt or powdered kelp
1 1/2 tsp. baking powder
1 tsp. lecithin granules
2 large eggs
2 T creamy style "natural" peanut butter
1 tsp. honey
1 c. water
1/3 c. powdered instant non-fat milk

1. Measure into a medium bowl the flour, sea salt or kelp, baking powder and lecithin.
2. In a small bowl, beat the eggs. Add the rest of the ingredients, each in order, beating after each addition.
3. Add liquid ingredients to dry, combining thoroughly with a wire whisk. Let the batter stand 15-20 minutes.
4. Bake on a hot seasoned griddle for 2-3 minutes, until the top is well bubbled and the sides are dry. Turn cakes and bake an additional 1-2 minutes, until the bottoms are golden.
5. Serve with butter and maple syrup.

_____

Milk allergic or just looking for something to zip up the morning?
Fruit juices can be used in place of milk to provide a refreshing change
of pace. Apple, orange, pineapple and cranberry juices, which go
especially well with whole grains, can substitute for milk in any recipe.
Because of their natural sweetness (excepting cranberry), fruit juices
eliminate the need for honey or any other sweetener in the batter.

Applejacks

Any flour can be used in place of wheat in this basic recipe for
fruit juice pancakes. Pastry wheat lets the apple flavor come out, so
that the applejacks taste like apple cakes. Hard wheat flour has a
more pronounced flavor of its own, but apple juice makes it sparkle.

For flour combinations and flours other than wheat, use 1 cup
total flour. Omit cinnamon if using orange, pineapple or cranberry
juice.

> 1 c. **pastry wheat flour**
>   OR 7/8 c. **hard wheat flour**
> 1/4 tsp. **sea salt or powdered kelp**
> 1 1/2 tsp. **baking powder**
> 1 tsp. **lecithin granules**
> 1/4 tsp. **cinnamon**
> 2 **whole eggs**
> 1 c. **pure apple juice (unsweetened)**
> 2 T. **cold pressed safflower oil**

1. Measure into a medium bowl, the flour, salt or kelp, baking powder,
lecithin and cinnamon.
2. In a small bowl, beat together the eggs, fruit juice and oil.
3. Combine liquid ingredients with dry. Bake on a hot seasoned
griddle as for Wheat Griddlecakes.
4. Serve these pancakes with any or all of the following: butter,
honey sweetened applesauce, cinnamon/apple sauce, maple syrup,
apple glaze and a dollop of yogurt.

Power Mix

Reach for your own Power Mix instead of all those other refined packaged batters. All you have to add to this super protein mix is egg and water. If you wish to double the milk protein, you can substitute whole milk for the water.

To make the mix

2 c. hard wheat flour
1/3 c. soy flour
1/2 c. wheat germ
1/3 c. powdered milk
2 T. baking powder
1 tsp. powdered kelp (or 3/4 tsp. sea salt)
1 T. lecithin granules

1. Combine in a medium bowl the wheat and soy flours, wheat germ, powdered milk, baking powder, kelp or salt, and lecithin.
2. Mix thoroughly and store, refrigerated, in a tightly lidded glass jar.

This mix will make 3 batches of pancakes for 2 persons.

To make the pancakes

2 eggs
1 c. water or 1 c. whole milk
2 1/2 T. cold pressed safflower oil
1 c. mix

1. Measure into a small bowl the eggs and water(or whole milk) and beat until blended.
2. Combine with the mix.
3. Bake as for Wheat Griddlecakes, page 66.

CORN MEAL, RICE FLOUR and GRAIN FLAKE CAKES _____

One of the finest ways to capture the aroma of freshly ground corn is to bake it into pancakes. However, the texture of corn meal calls for a different handling of the batter from regular whole grain pancakes. Home milled corn meal offers not only freshness but nutritional superiority over store bought corn meal. Most commercial varieties have the germ removed (degerminated) for better storage, since the corn germ, like wheat germ, will rapidly go rancid if the meal is not refrigerated.

There are several varieties of ground corn on supermarket shelves—stone ground, water ground, and masa. Stone ground corn meals may or may not be degerminated—read the label carefully! Water ground, on the other hand, means that the process of milling has retained the germ. Masa is corn that has been soaked in lime water (in a process similar to the lye soaking of hominy) and the bran layer has been removed.

Ground corn can range from coarse meal to a fine powder or flour. You can choose the setting on your home grinder to suit your preference. Twice through a steel hand mill is sufficient for almost any recipe, especially if the second setting is drawn down tight. The best results for pancakes is a fine meal. You can feel the graininess of the corn when you rub a small quantity of the meal between your fingers. It is this characteristic graininess of ground corn that requires a pre-soaking step in making pancakes.

Rice flour ground from long or short grain brown rice, is also grainy in texture. When ground at home, brown rice does not resemble commercially produced flour, which is fine and powdery as a result of high heat and processing speeds. Consequently, rice flour used in pancakes takes the same treatment as corn, pre-soaking.

For a novel and soon to be repeated breakfast, try the pre-soak method on your favorite cereal flakes or combination of flakes. Oat flakes (rolled oats) absorb moisture more readily than any other cereal flake, and they are more tender in the finished pancake. In contrast, wheat flakes retain their chewiness even after soaking, and resemble softened wheat berries in a delicious bed of batter. Rye, triticale and barley flakes likewise make delicious and interestingly textured pancakes.

The pilot recipe (Corn Cakes) calls for 1/3 cup of pastry flour, since corn alone cannot hold the rise of the pancake, which will collapse without the addition of another flour. Rice and grain flakes perform similarly. Pastry wheat has been selected for these pancakes because it allows the flavor of corn, rice, or flake to dominate. Hard wheat flour can be substituted, decreasing the amount to 1/4 cup, although it will lend its own distinctive flavor. Wheat flour is not an absolute: 1/3 cup of oat, barley, rye, buckwheat or triticale can be used instead. For example, a whole oat pancake would use 1/2 cup rolled oats and 1/3 cup oat flour. Make sure the griddle is *hot* for a well crowned cake.

Corn Cakes

Serve with butter, maple syrup and 1/2 c. double rich yogurt to boost these cakes up to 18.5 g. protein per serving.

1/2 c. fine corn meal
1/4 tsp. sea salt or powdered kelp
1 tsp. lecithin granules
1/2 c. boiling water
1 tsp. honey or 1 T. pure maple syrup
1 whole egg
1/4 c. water
3 T. powdered instant non-fat milk
1 T. cold pressed safflower or corn oil
1/3 c. whole wheat pastry flour
1 tsp. baking powder

1. In a medium bowl, measure and mix the corn meal, salt or kelp, and lecithin.
2. Add the boiling water and sweetener, stir. Cover and let this mixture stand for 20 minutes.
3. Heat the griddle.
4. In a small bowl or dish, combine the egg, water, milk and oil.
5. Add the egg/milk mixture to the soaked cornmeal.
6. Mix in a small bowl the pastry flour and baking powder. Quickly stir the flour/baking powder mixture into the cornmeal/egg mixture.
7. Bake on a hot, well seasoned griddle until the tops are bubbly and the sides are beginning to dry (2 minutes). Turn and bake until the undersides are brown (an additional 1 minute).

Barleycorn Cakes

Follow the recipe for Corn Cakes, substituting 1/3 c. of barley flour for 1/3 c. whole wheat pastry flour.

Rice Cakes

These are sweet thin pancakes that go well with fruit sauces and glazes, especially raspberry. Those who love their maple syrup should sprinkle toasted sesame seeds on the finished cakes for a delicious protein complement.

Follow the recipe for Corn Cakes, substituting 1/2 cup brown rice flour (steel or stone ground) for 1/2 cup corn meal called for in the recipe, and increasing the pastry flour to 1/2 cup.

Rolled Oat Cakes

They are tender, mildly sweet and ever so slightly chewy. Serve them any way your taste buds dictate. They are good enough to stand alone.

For a complete oat cake, use 1/3 c. oat flour in place of the 1/3 c. whole wheat pastry flour.

    1/2 c. rolled oats
    1/8 tsp. sea salt or 1/4 tsp. powdered kelp
    1 tsp. lecithin granules
    1/2 c. boiling water
    1 tsp. raw unfiltered honey
    1 whole egg
    1/4 c. water
    3 T. powdered instant non-fat milk
    1 T. cold pressed safflower oil
    1/3 C. whole wheat pastry flour
    1 tsp. baking powder

1. In a medium bowl measure and mix the oats, salt or kelp, and lecithin.
2. Add the boiling water and honey. Stir.
3. Cover and let this mixture stand for 20 minutes.
4. Heat the griddle. Beat and add to soaked oats the egg, water, milk and oil.
5. In a small dish, combine the pastry flour and baking powder.
6. Rapidly stir the dry ingredients into the wet ingredients until barely combined.
7. Fry on a hot seasoned griddle until the tops are bubbly and the sides are beginning to dry (about 2 minutes). Turn and continue baking until undersides are brown (1 more minute).

Wheat Flake Cakes

Wheat flakes are usually thicker than oat flakes and do not absorb moisture as quickly or as evenly. Twenty minutes of soaking will leave the wheat flakes still chewy—a welcome change in pancake texture. Think of the flakes as "instant" soaked wheat berries.

Follow the recipe for Rolled Oat Cakes, substituting 1/2 cup wheat flakes for 1/2 cup rolled oats. When ladling onto the griddle, the batter holding the soaked flakes will appear thin, but it will firm up nicely upon cooking. Since wheat flakes have a tendency to clump more than oat flakes, be sure to distribute the flakes evenly across the pancake when pouring the batter onto the griddle.

Triticale Flake Cakes

Follow the recipe for Rolled Oat Cakes, substituting 1/2 c. triticale flakes for 1/2 c. rolled oats. For 100% triticale pancakes, use 1/3 c. triticale flour in place of the 1/3 c. whole wheat pastry flour.

Rye Flake Cakes

Follow the recipe for Rolled Oat Cakes, substituting 1/2 cup rye flakes for 1/2 cup rolled oats. Because the flavor is strong, it is best combined with another grain. If you want a break from wheat, try barley or oat flour in place of the 1/3 cup whole wheat pastry flour.

Rolled Barley Cakes

Follow the recipe for Rolled Oat Cakes, substituting 1/2 cup rolled barley for 1/2 cup rolled oats. For 100% barley cakes, use 1/3 cup barley flour in place of the 1/3 cup whole wheat pastry flour. Any other finely ground flour may be used in place of the whole wheat pastry flour.

Flat Pancakes

Crepes

Crepes are basically very thin pancakes that take no leavening. They can be glazed, rolled, filled, or wrapped around a slice of fruit. Since they do not rise in the pan, crepes are the most versatile of all pancakes. Any grain—even legumes—can be turned into a crepe, since the binding ingredient in the batter is the whole egg. Flours such as corn and rice that do not hold up well by themselves in stack cakes make excellent crepes. Likewise, triticale and oat, the softer flours, make tender, delicious crepes.

Crepe batters generally call for milk or milk solids, but fruit juices used in place of milk result in crepes with a new zest. Apple and orange juices perk up any crepe recipe.

The following recipes are all pilot recipes—other flours or liquids can be substituted as taste and diet desire. Use fruit sauces liberally when serving crepes. Spread the sauce over the bottom of the flat crepe, then roll. Top with a dollop of fresh yogurt and you have a refreshing, protein packed crepe.

Wheat and oat flours make the most tender crepes. When frying up a batch, stack them gently in an ovenproof dish. Cover them with a tea towel to keep them warm for serving. If you are making several batches of crepes, keep the covered dish in a warming oven or main oven set on low temperature. Be careful. As crepes dry out, they get tough. A great part of the delight in eating these pancakes is their tenderness, their "melt-in-the-mouth" quality. A good crepe should be somewhat elastic.

There are any number of crepe pans on the market which, while handy, are not necessary. I have always used two 8 inch cast iron skillets. (The 8 inch is the manufacturer's measurement from rim to rim; the bottom of the pan actually makes a 6 inch crepe.) Once seasoned, a cast iron pan offers steady, uniform heat and requires only a drop or two of oil between crepes. Cast iron cookware also imparts the nutritional bonus of iron to the food that is cooked in it; most people can use this mineral in greater quantity.

Crepes may sound like work, but in the long run they are a time saver. There is no need to separate the eggs. Moreover, the batter only improves while you tend to other morning chores. The crepes cook rapidly and the cast iron pans need only to be wiped clean. Any extras can be frozen and quickly thawed in the oven when you need them. They hold up well in storage, even in the refrigerator.

Try your own combination of grains. Make Wheat/Oat or Buckwheat/Barley crepes. Just make sure that the total volume of flour equals 3/4 cup for all grains other than hard whole wheat. One hundred percent whole wheat crepes made from hard wheat absorb more moisture and require less flour— 2/3 cup. When combining hard wheat with any other grain, however, follow the recipe for pastry crepes and keep to the 1 cup total measure.

Corn, rice and garbanzo flours require pre-soaking in boiling water to soften the hard particles of grain and to "pre-cook" the bean. These crepes are more hearty than those made from the softer grain flours, making for a change of pace. Try sprinkling them with cheese before rolling and topping them with pineapple sauce.

Pastry Crepes

3/4 c. whole wheat pastry flour
1/8 tsp. sea salt or powdered kelp
1 tsp. lecithin granules
3 whole eggs
1 c. water
1/2 c. powdered instant non-fat milk

1. In a medium bowl, measure and mix the pastry flour, salt or kelp, and lecithin.
2. In a small bowl, whisk together the eggs, water and milk.
3. Pour the liquid ingredients into the dry and beat thoroughly with a wire whisk. Cover the bowl (a luncheon plate usually works fine) and let stand from 15 minutes to an hour. This resting period gives the grain time to absorb moisture and produces an even textured crepe. Stir again before cooking.
4. Heat a crepe pan or 2 to 3 cast iron skillets. The quantity of crepes will vary depending on the size of the skillets. If the bottom measures 6 inches, the batter will yield around 18 thin pancakes.

If the pans are well seasoned, there will be no need to oil them for the first crepe or two. If the pans appear dry, drop in a few drops of cold pressed safflower oil and swirl them around. Holding the handle of one skillet at a time, ladle a small amount of batter in the center of the pan and swirl the pan around so that the batter just covers the bottom. After a few crepes, you will be able to judge just how much batter to put in. It is a fine line between too much batter and too little, but in either case, the crepe will still be edible. If you have not put in enough batter, quickly add more and swirl the pan. If you have poured in too much, resign yourself to a thick and indelicate crepe. Keep practicing your technique—mastery may be only a crepe away.

Cook the crepes over moderately high heat. When using two pans, you will be pouring and turning constantly, since the batter cooks quickly. As soon as the top appears dry—1-2 minutes—turn the crepe and let it cook in the skillet only long enough to brown the underside. Most of the cooking is done before turning. Run a metal spatula around the edges of the crepe to loosen it from the pan. The edges are always thin and may tend to stick to the sides of the pan where there is the least oil. Then insert the spatula under the center of the crepe and turn. When the underside is brown (30 seconds to 1 minute), transfer the crepe to a warm dish or plate. Cover with a tea towel and tend to the rest of the batter.

Pastry crepes are complemented by any fruit sauce or filling. As with all crepes, spread a tablespoon or more of filling on the flat crepe, then roll. The filling may be fruit, nut butter spreads, yogurt or grated cheese. The number of garnishes is limited only by the imagination. Date or maple sugar sprinkled on the crepe before rolling are often enough, but don't hesitate to add a yogurt topping and some chopped nuts or toasted sesame seeds.

Graham Crepes

These are called "Graham" as distinct from Pastry Crepes because they are made with hard wheat—either spring or winter type. The same amount of moisture handles less hard wheat flour than pastry flour. Hence, the basic recipe is adjusted as follows.

Graham Crepes maintain the full bodied flavor of wheat, at its best when freshly ground and griddled.

2/3 c. hard wheat flour
1/8 tsp. sea salt or powdered kelp
1 tsp. lecithin granules
3 whole eggs
1 c. water
1/2 c. powdered instant non-fat milk

1. Into a medium bowl, combine the flour, salt or kelp, and lecithin.
2. In a small bowl, measure and whisk together the eggs, water and milk.
3. Combine liquid ingredients with dry and whisk thoroughly. Cover and let stand 20 minutes to 1 hour.
4. Cook as for Pastry Crepes, page 88.

100% Barley Crepes

Follow the recipe for Pastry Crepes, page 88, using 3/4 cup barley flour (ground from whole barley in a steel or stone mill) in place of the pastry wheat flour.

Because barley is sweeter than wheat, it goes well with any fruit sauce.

100% Buckwheat Crepes

Follow the recipe for Pastry Crepes, page 88, but use 3/4 cup ground sprouting buckwheat with hulls or ground buckwheat groats in place of the pastry wheat. If a sprouting buckwheat is used, the crepes will be a bit drier. Make sure to grind the buckwheat as fine as possible to break up the hulls.

Serve with date, fig or raisin sauce.

Nut Crepes

To any recipe, add up to 1/4 cup ground cashews, ground sesame seeds or sunflower meal. Finely ground pecans, walnuts, and almonds can also be added in the same amount.

100% Rye Crepes

Follow the recipe for Pastry Crepes, page 88, using 3/4 c. whole rye flour (ground from rye berries the same way you would grind wheat berries) in place of the pastry wheat flour.

Serve with fig, date or raisin sauce.

Soy Wheat Crepes

High protein soy flour combines best with the distinctive flavor of hard wheat. Serve with date or raisin sauce.

Spoon into a 1 cup measure 2 T. full fat soy flour. Fill to 2/3 c. level with hard wheat flour. Use this mixture as the flour component and proceed as for Graham Crepes, page 90.

100% Triticale Crepes

Follow the recipe for Pastry Crepes, page 88, using 3/4 cup triticale flour (ground from whole triticale as you would grind wheat berries) in place of the pastry wheat flour.

Wheat Germ Crepes

The flavor of wheat germ seems to combine best with its natural companion, whole wheat flour.

Spoon into a 1 cup measure 3 T. wheat germ. Fill to 2/3 level with hard wheat flour. Proceed as for Graham Crepes, page 90.

Peanut Butter Crepes

Peanut butter boosts the protein in any crepe recipe by complementing both the grain and the milk proteins. Variations in the basic peanut butter crepe can be made by substituting 3/4 cup of any other grain in place of the wheat.

3/4 c. whole wheat pastry flour
   OR 2/3 c. hard wheat flour
1/8 tsp. sea salt or powdered kelp
1 tsp. lecithin granules
3 whole eggs
1/4 c. creamy style "natural" peanut butter
   OR homemade peanut butter
1 c. water
1/2 c. powdered instant non-fat milk

1. Into a medium bowl, measure either kind of whole wheat flour, the salt or kelp, and lecithin.
2. In a small bowl, beat the eggs. Add the peanut butter, whisking until smooth.
3. Gradually incorporate the water and milk.
4. Blend the liquid ingredients with dry.
5. Proceed as for Pastry Crepes, page 88.

Carob Crepes

This surprising variation is doubly good with carob sauce or maple syrup. Yogurt or peanut butter spread make good garnishes or fillers.

3 T. carob flour
3/4 c. minus 3 T. whole wheat pastry flour
1/4 tsp. cinnamon
1/8 tsp. sea salt or powdered kelp
1 tsp. lecithin granules
3 whole eggs
1 c. water
1/2 c. powdered instant non-fat milk

1. Spoon the carob into a 1 cup measure. Fill to 3/4 c. level with the flour. Transfer to a medium bowl and add cinnamon, salt or kelp and lecithin.
2. Proceed as for Pastry Crepes, page 88.

Oat Crepes

This wheat-free pancake should be at the top of everyone's list for flavor, texture, high protein and low calories. A sweet crepe, it goes well with any fruit sauce filling or just plain bananas, sliced or mashed, drizzled with honey and topped with yogurt. A dab af peanut butter with the bananas is even better.

Follow the recipe for Pastry Crepes, page 88, but use 3/4 cup oat flour in place of the 3/4 c. pastry flour. For home ground oat flour, use whole oat groats in a steel or stone mill and grind as for wheat berries or place rolled oats in the blender, 1 cup at a time, and process at "grind" until they are powdered.

Oat crepes are open to a wide array of variations. Make them into peanut butter crepes by adding 1/4 cup creamy peanut butter to the recipe. Or sprinkle the pan with raw unhulled sesame seeds or dried, shredded coconut. Make Carob/Oat crepes by measuring 3 T. carob flour into the bottom of the measuring cup and filling to 3/4 cup level with oat flour.

Snap Apple Crepes

Pure apple juice in place of milk makes these crepes even more delicate than regular Pastry Crepes, so be careful to watch the crepe pan, making sure that it is well seasoned for each crepe. A drop or two of oil added to the pan between crepes will keep them from sticking.

Serve with pure maple syrup, nothing more.

    3/4 c. whole wheat pastry flour
      OR oat flour
    1/4 tsp. cinnamon
    1/8 tsp. sea salt or powdered kelp
    1 tsp. lecithin granules
    3 whole eggs
    1 c. apple juice

1. Into a medium bowl, measure and combine the flour, cinnamon, salt or kelp, and lecithin.
2. Whisk together in a small bowl the eggs and juice.
3. Combine liquid with dry ingredients and let stand. Cook as for Pastry Crepes, page 88.

Chunky Apple Crepes

Chunky apple crepes are a variation of regular Pastry Crepes. Their apple flavor comes from the fruit itself.

Prepare the batter for Pastry Crepes, page 88, adding 1 T. pure maple syrup and 1 medium apple, cored and finely chopped.

Proceed as for Pastry Crepes.

Flapjacks

These thin corn crepes require a pre-soak period to soften up the cornmeal. They can be made from white or yellow corn, preferably ground to a fine meal at home and used fresh or refrigerated immediately after grinding. If you buy corn meal ground commercially, make sure that the germ and bran layers have been retained. Read the label.

3/4 c. fine corn meal
1/8 tsp. sea salt or powdered kelp
1 tsp. lecithin granules
1 c. boiling water
3 whole eggs
1/2 c. water
1/2 c. powdered instant non-fat milk

1. Into a medium bowl, measure the corn meal, salt or kelp, and lecithin.
2. Pour the boiling water over the meal mixture. Stir, cover and let stand for 20 minutes.
3. In a small bowl, beat together the eggs, water and milk.
4. Whisk the beaten egg/milk mixture into the corn meal until the batter is smooth.
5. The crepes can be cooked immediately, since the corn meal has already been soaked. Heat the crepe pan or cast iron skillet, pour in a small amount of batter and swirl as for Pastry Crepes, page 88.

Flapjacks may require a drop or two of oil in the pan between each crepe. Serve piping hot with pure maple syrup or sprinkle with grated cheddar cheese before rolling and then top with pineapple sauce.

This recipe yields 18 crepes or approximately 2 servings.

Rice Thins

Follow the recipe for Flapjacks, page 97, using 3/4 cup finely ground brown rice flour in place of the corn meal. Brown rice ground at home is grainy and, like corn, requires a pre-soak period. When cooked into crepes, rice flour becomes chewier than other whole grain flours. Raspberry glaze is a must, though pure maple syrup will do.

Cicero's Crepe

Yes, it's possible—a thin pancake made from a bean. The mild flavored garbanzo bean, or *Cicer,* makes for a high protein crepe. A novel way to eat breakfast beans!

Chickpea flour (Indian *besan*), is available commercially, but the peas can be ground easily in a steel mill. On the first run through, crack the beans as you would corn; then draw down the adjustment knob for fine flour the second time through.

1/2 c. chickpea flour
1/8 tsp. sea salt or powdered kelp
1 tsp. lecithin granules
1 c. boiling water
3 whole eggs
1/2 c. water
1/2 c. powdered instant non-fat milk

1. Into a small bowl, measure the flour, salt or kelp, and lecithin.
2. Pour boiling water over these ingredients.
3. Let stand for a half hour and proceed as for Flapjacks, page 97.

Blintzes

A blintz is a crepe filled with cheese and sauteed in butter. Any crepe can fill in for a blintz, but the standard against which all flavors are measured is the Pastry Crepe, page 88.

Make one batch of Pastry Crepes. This will yield 18-20 thin pancakes, or enough to serve 2 persons for breakfast for 2 days (4 servings in all). The crepes may be filled after they have been cooked and cooled, or they may be rolled the following day. However, any crepes that have been filled should be sauteed immediately, since the water in the filling will "weep" into the crepe unless the crepe is re-cooked. Leftover sauteed blintzes can be stored refrigerated and reheated the following morning.

    1 c. uncreamed cottage cheese, ricotta or homemade cheese
    1 beaten egg
    (1/4 tsp. orange or lemon zest)*

1. Combine the cheese, egg and peel (optional) for a filling.
2. Place 2 T. filling in the center of each crepe. Fold over the side edges as for an envelope, then roll. Place the seam side down in a lightly buttered skillet. Saute over medium heat until golden, then turn and saute the other side. Serve the warm blintzes with yogurt and fruit sauce. Sprinkle with chopped nuts.

---

* "Zest" is ground dried citrus peel. To make your own, slice clean peels thinly, dry in fresh circulating air on a wire mesh or screen, then store in clean glass jars. Pulverize the dried peels with a mortar and pestle or blender just before using.

Swedish Pancakes

Milk is the major ingredient of these Scandinavian cakes, which blend in just enough egg to bind the batter. Somewhat thicker than crepes, Swedish pancakes are still thin enough to roll, and traditionally they are served that way, under a ladle full of lingonberry sauce and a peak of fresh sour cream. You can easily duplicate the treat by preparing your own lingonberry sauce with honey and substituting fresh thick yogurt for the sour cream.

Here are some other serving ideas, all topped with yogurt:
1) Fill each pancake with chopped fresh fruit and then roll.
2) Spread the pancakes with fruit puree or mashed bananas and then roll.
3) Roll plain and pour on stewed fruits or fresh fruit compote.
4) Roll plain and drizzle with maple syrup.
5) Roll plain and top with fruit sauce. Sprinkle nuts, Crunchy Wheat Germ or granola over the yogurt.
6) Spread with honey-sweetened peanut butter, roll, then drizzle lightly with pure maple syrup.
7) Spread with any of the above and stack, like a seven layer cake.

Because there is a smaller quantity of whole grain flour and only 1 egg in the batter, it is important to serve the pancakes with yogurt to maximize the protein content of the breakfast. Another way of boosting nutrition is to incorporate chopped nuts or seeds into the batter. Fruit juice used in place of water will add valuable minerals, but be sure to add the milk solids as well unless another protein source will accompany the rolled cakes. The omission of milk solids will require a subsequent reduction in the measure of water to 3/4 cup. However, then the pancakes begin to enter the domain of the crepe. The particular texture of a Swedish pancake is achieved by one egg and a large proportion of milk to flour, and any alteration of that proportion, however appealing or nutritionally sound, will produce a different texture and consequently, a different pancake.

Be sure to use a flat griddle; some electric frypans are slightly concave while some cast iron griddles are crowned. The batter for each of these pancake recipes will be thin and will run before it sets if the griddle is inclined in any direction.

Define the boundaries of each pancake by ladling the batter in a round circle, pouring the outside edge of the pancake and working in a concentric circular motion to the center. This may sound very exacting, but it is actually accomplished in one quick movement. It is also possible to ladle onto the griddle at the centerpoint of each pancake, provided you are satisfied with less than perfect rounds.

The griddle should be hot and well-seasoned. One light initial coat of oil should be enough to cook a batch of pancakes.

Be versatile and imaginative. Make use of the fruits the land is known for, whether they are cultivated or wild. Plan ahead during the growing season to put up enough fruits for winter sauces.

The Swedish Cake
(Basic)

1 whole egg
1 c. water (room temperature)
1/2 c. powdered instant non-fat milk
1/8 tsp. sea salt
1 tsp. lecithin granules
1/2 c. hard wheat flour
2 T. raw wheat germ
2 tsp. cold pressed safflower oil
1 tsp. raw unfiltered honey

1. Into a medium bowl, measure and whisk together, in order: the egg, water, milk, salt, lecithin, flour, wheat germ, oil and honey. Whisk together until smooth and let stand for 15 minutes.
2. Lightly oil the hot griddle. Using a ladle or quarter cup measure, pour the batter onto the cooking surface. The tops will bubble and the batter will be set when it is time to turn the pancakes, usually 1 minute. Flip, then cook an additional 1/2 minute. Since these pancakes cook fast, you will want to make the whole batch before serving. To keep them hot and pliable, place the pancakes on a warmed plate as they are done and cover them with foil. Layer them on the plate until the entire batter has been cooked. Steam from the bottom pancakes will rise through the top pancakes, thus keeping them all moist, warm and ready to roll.

Makes sixteen 4 inch pancakes.

Swedish Wheat Soy Cakes

Soy mixed with wheat makes an excellent pancake, with hearty flavor and texture. Follow the recipe for the Basic Swedish Cake, substituting 2 T. soy flour for the wheat germ.

Swedish Oat Cakes

Oat pancakes complement any flavor of filling. These thin pancakes are good spread with fruit puree and topped with yogurt or rolled plain and drizzled with syrup.

Oat flour can also be used in other recipes in place of wheat flour for those on a wheat-free diet. In this recipe, if wheat germ cannot be tolerated, increase the oat flour by 2 T.

Follow the recipe for the Basic Swedish Cake, substituting 1/2 c. oat flour (ground from oat groats or rolled oats) for the whole wheat flour.

Swedish Oat Soy Cakes

Follow the recipe for the Basic Swedish Cake, using 1/2 c. oat flour plus 2 T. soy flour in place of the whole wheat and wheat germ.

Swedish Carob Cakes

Follow the recipe for the Basic Swedish Cake, substituting 1/2 c. soft wheat flour for the hard wheat flour and 2 T. carob flour for the wheat germ.

Maple syrup and yogurt are all you need for these.

Swedish Corn Cakes

Corn is usually combined with wheat in pancake recipes, but as this recipe proves, it makes a fine pancake all by itself. Use this recipe for Swedish Rice Cakes, substituting brown rice flour for the corn meal.

1/2 c. fine corn meal
1/2 c. boiling water
1 egg
1/4 c. water (room temperature)
1/2 c. powdered instant non-fat milk
1 tsp. lecithin granules
1/8 tsp. sea salt
2 tsp. cold pressed safflower oil
1 tsp. maple syrup or honey

1. Stir together the corn meal and boiling water until all the meal is moistened. Let cool to room temperature.
2. In a medium bowl, beat the egg.
3. Add, beating (or whisking) the moistened corn meal, water, milk, lecithin, salt, oil and sweetener. Combine thoroughly.
4. Let stand for 15 minutes. Bake on a hot griddle.
5. Spread with date puree, roll, then top with fresh yogurt.

Swedish Peanut Cakes

One-quarter cup of peanut butter produces a lightly flavored pancake. To bring out the flavor, add more chopped roasted peanuts to the combined batter.

1 egg
1/4 c. natural peanut butter (crunchy or smooth. If peanut butter is salted, omit salt from the batter)
1 c. water
1/2 c. powdered instant non-fat milk
1 tsp. lecithin granules
1/8 tsp. sea salt
1 tsp. cold pressed safflower or peanut oil
1 tsp. honey

1. Into a medium bowl, beat the egg.
2. Add, beating in order, the peanut butter, water, milk, lecithin, salt, oil and honey.
3. Bake as for Basic Swedish Pancakes, page 102.
4. Spread with honeyed peanut butter. Roll, cover generously with a berry sauce, then top with yogurt for a breakfast variation of peanut butter and jelly.

Swedish Pancake Variations

Play your hunches and heed your taste buds. There is still triticale, barley/oat, barley/rye, barley/wheat, wheat/rye, buckwheat/wheat, barley/soy, rye/soy, corn/oat, triticale/oat and every combination of those with wheat germ and/or bran waiting to be tried.

Oven Pancakes

Oven pancakes are midway between omelettes and custards or souffles, since they rely upon the eggs to provide a lift to the batter, which is light on flour. Almost all of the old recipes for oven pancakes had a uniform texture produced by the refined flour. No matter how much you beat the eggs or measure the milk, an oven pancake made with home ground whole wheat will separate into two distinct layers: custard on top and a cereal pudding on the bottom. There are several ways around this dilemma, however: 1) omit wheat flour altogether and use arrowroot, 2) use wheat flour, but bake the pancakes in skillet size pans, 3) use finely ground oat flour.

The following sampler recipes guarantee uniform texture in easy-to-prepare pancakes.

Pancake Souffle

A wheatless breakfast treat that assembles quickly and becomes elegant with warm pineapple or orange sauce.

4 eggs
1 T. raw unfiltered honey
3 T. powdered instant non-fat milk
1/2 c. water
2 T. arrowroot
1 tsp. lecithin granules
1/2 tsp. orange zest
1 T. butter

1. Into two medium bowls, separate the eggs.
2. Warm the honey, milk and water slightly, then whisk into the yolks.
3. Add arrowroot, lecithin and zest to the yolk mixture.
4. Beat the 4 egg whites until stiff, then fold the yolk mixture into the beaten whites.
5. In a 400 degrees F. oven, melt the butter in a 1 quart casserole, baking or souffle dish.
6. Turn the batter into the hot baking dish and bake 5 minutes at 400 degrees F. then reduce the heat to 374 F. and bake an additional 15-20 minutes, until puffed, golden and set.
7. Serve immediately, with or without fruit sauce, as the pancake souffle will fall upon cooling.

As an alternate to fruit sauces, garnish with maple sugar and chopped walnuts.

Serves two.

Variation
Substitute 2 T. carob flour for arrowroot flour, and serve with honey, maple syrup or date sauce.

Fruit Pancakes

Cheese, fruit, whole wheat and eggs combine to make a high protein, high mineral breakfast.

Use fruit juice in place of water and add milk solids. Or use fruit juice in place of water and omit milk solids. Substitute various whole grain flours for wheat pastry flour. Serve with matching or complementary fruit sauces. Make one large pancake (10-12 inch skillet) and split it for two, or make two 6 inch pancakes and serve individually.

> 3 eggs
> 1/3 c. naturally sweet fruit juice, such as apple,
>   orange or pineapple*
>   OR
>   1/3 c. water plus 2 T. powdered instant non-fat milk
> 2 T. raw unfiltered honey
> 1/3 c. whole wheat pastry flour
> 1 tsp. lecithin granules
> 1 1/2 T. butter
> 1 c. cheddar cheese

1. In a medium bowl, beat the eggs.
2. Add the fruit juice (or water plus powdered milk) and the honey, flour and lecithin.
3. In a 450 degree F. oven, melt 1 1/2 T butter in a 10-12 inch heavy skillet or 3/4 T. butter in each of two 6 inch baking pans or skillets.
4. Pour the batter into the hot skillet(s) and bake for 12 minutes, until puffed and golden.
5. While the pancake is baking, grate the cheddar cheese.
6. Sprinkle the cheese over the cooked pancakes(s), return to the oven until the cheese is melted, then roll the pancakes(s).
7. Serve topped with a generous serving of cinnamon/applesauce, pineapple sauce or rhubarb sauce.**

Serves two.

* When using apple juice, add 1/4 tsp. cinnamon to the batter. Serve with cinnamon flavored applesauce. When using pineapple juice, add 1 tsp. lemon juice to the batter. Serve with pineapple sauce.
** When serving with rhubarb sauce, make the recipe with water plus milk solids.

Blender Pancakes

Blender pancakes are nothing short of magic. A blender, when accessible, eliminates the need for grinding grains into flours and makes pancakes only one step from the whole grain or seed to the batter. No pancake could contain fresher vitamins or minerals than the pancake made from the whole grain with all its nutrients intact right up to the moment of mixing.

Since power is a rare commodity in Alaska, my blender is reserved for accomplishing what cannot be accomplished by hand. Whole berries, nuts and seeds may be pre-soaked and blended. The problem of grinding soy beans to flour in any mill but a steel mill is also solved by the blender. The beans need not be ground at all. Just pre-soak and blend them whole!

Overnight soaking of grains is recommended, but it is not necessary. The soaking softens the grain enough to make the grinding easier on the blender and to produce a smooth batter. Unsoaked grains can be gritty, because they have not had time to absorb moisture, although occasionally such textures are desirable (in corn pancakes, for example). Since you will be using the soaking water as the liquid component of the batter, do not think of the pre-soaking as an extra chore. Rather, if you measure the grain and water into the blender the night before, breakfast preparation will only be a matter of adding the other ingredients and turning on the blender.

The blender makes possible a whole range of grain combinations that produce superbly textured pancakes. Pre-soaking, then rapid blending seems to work up normally crumbly grains into cohesive batters that hold their rise well. Oats and barley are good examples.

Grain flakes can be used in place of whole grains, but be sure to increase their measure. If one-third cup of whole grains are called for, use a scant two-thirds cup of cereal flakes. Since the flaking process means steaming and rolling, flakes do not need to be pre-soaked, but can be added directly to the batter before blending in the morning.

Blender Wheat Cakes

These are springy like yeast cakes, but with the fragrance of freshly milled wheat. Use either hard or soft wheat, according to taste preference. The liquid measure remains the same for either variety.

2/3 c. whole wheat berries
1 c. water (room temperature)
2 whole eggs
3 T. cold pressed safflower oil
1/4 tsp. sea salt
1 tsp. lecithin granules
1 T. raw unfiltered honey
1/2 c. powdered instant non-fat milk
1 1/2 tsp. baking powder

1. The night before, soak the wheat berries in water.
2. In the morning, add the eggs, oil, salt, lecithin and honey.
3. Process at blend or grind until the batter is smooth. You may have to scrape down the sides of the blender container with a rubber spatula to be sure that all of the wheat berries are ground into the batter.
4. When it is smooth and creamy in appearance, add gradually, while blending, the milk and baking powder.
5. When the milk and baking powder are thoroughly incorporated, turn the blender off and let the batter stand for 20-30 minutes before baking the pancakes.
6. During this time, heat the griddle.

Wheat cakes take a hot seasoned griddle. After the initial set of cakes have been poured, little, if any, additional oil will be needed on the griddle.

7. Pour the batter from the blender onto the griddle. Bake until the tops are well bubbled and the sides are dry (1 1/2 - 2 minutes). Flip and bake until the undersides are well-browned, about 45 seconds to 1 minute more.
8. Pure maple syrup and butter are hard to beat, although a dollop of yogurt makes for a nutritious and taste complementing bonus.

Makes sixteen 3 1/2 - 4 inch pancakes.

The following 7 recipes are variations on the basic Blender Wheat Cake recipe.

Blender Wheat Oat Cakes

These cakes are nutty and sweet—a perfect blend of flavors.

1/3 c. hard wheat berries
1/3 c. oat groats
1 c. water
2 whole eggs
3 T. cold pressed safflower oil
1/4 tsp. sea salt
1 tsp. lecithin granules
1 T. raw unfiltered honey
1/2 c. powdered instant non-fat milk
1 1/2 tsp. baking powder

1. Pre-soak the wheat berries and oats in water.
2. The next morning follow the directions for Blender Wheat Cakes.

Rolled oats can be used instead of oat groats. However, they produce a pancake somewhat heavier in texture and chewier. Pre-soak 1/3 c. hard wheat berries in 1 c. water. In the morning add 2/3 c. rolled oats and proceed as for Blender Wheat Cakes.

Blender Bran Cakes

Surprisingly light pancakes. Fine particles of bran and shreds of wheat have the texture of coconut.

> 1/2 c. hard wheat berries
> 1 c. water
> 1/3 c. miller's bran (raw, unprocessed bran)
> 2 whole eggs
> 3 T. cold pressed safflower oil
> 1/4 tsp. sea salt
> 1 tsp. lecithin granules
> 1 T. raw unfiltered honey
> 1/2 c. powdered instant non-fat milk
> 1 1/2 tsp. baking powder

1. Pre-soak the wheat in water.
2. In the morning, add the bran.
3. Proceed as for Blender Wheat Cakes, page 110.

Variation

For a nutritional boost, substitute raw wheat germ for part of the bran. Should you find yourself enjoying the wheat germ flavor, use it in place of the full 1/3 c. of bran to make Blender Wheat Germ Cakes.

Blender Carob Cakes

No carob or chocolate aficionado can afford to pass up these.

1/2 c. soft wheat berries
3/4 c. water
1/4 c. carob flour
(1/2 tsp. cinnamon)
2 whole eggs
3 T. cold pressed safflower oil
1/4 tsp. sea salt
1 tsp. lecithin granules
1 T. raw unfiltered honey
1/2 c. powdered instant non-fat milk
1 1/2 tsp. baking powder

1. Pre-soak the wheat berries in water.
2. In the morning, add the carob and cinnamon.
3. Proceed as for Blender Wheat Cakes, page 110.

Blender Nutty Wheat Cakes

This basic recipe calls for sunflower seeds, but roasted peanuts, raw or roasted cashews, almonds, millet, walnuts, pumpkin seeds, brazil nuts, filberts or pecans make equally delicious pancakes.

Should you be trying to avoid wheat, use oat groats in place of wheat berries, or experiment with barley and rye.

1/2 c. hard wheat berries
1 c. water
1/4 c. raw hulled sunflower seeds
2 whole eggs
3 T. cold pressed safflower oil
1/4 tsp. sea salt
1 tsp. lecithin granules
1 T. raw unfiltered honey
1/2 c. powdered instant non-fat milk
1 1/2 tsp. baking powder

1. Pre-soak the wheat berries in water.
2. In the morning, add the sunflower seeds.
3. Proceed as for Blender Wheat Cakes, page 110.

Blender Corn Cakes

Since dried corn is slow to absorb moisture, it benefits from all the pre-conditioning it can get. Ground to a fine flour, as in this recipe, it can be added directly to the batter, and the fine particles will soften in the half-hour standing period. If you have access only to coarse corn meal, mix it with 1/2 c. boiling water before adding to the blender. The soaking water for the wheat or oat groats would consequently be reduced to 1/2 c., so that the total for the pancakes equals 1 cup.

White or yellow, corn always makes an aromatic pancake when it meets the griddle. These cakes are simply delicious.

    1/3 c. soft wheat berries or oat groats
    1 c. water
    1/2 c. corn flour
    2 whole eggs
    3 T. cold pressed safflower oil
    1/4 tsp. sea salt
    1 tsp. lecithin granules
    1 T. raw unfiltered honey
    1/2 c. powdered instant non-fat milk
    1 1/2 tsp. baking powder

1. Pre-soak the wheat or oats in water.
2. In the morning, add the corn flour.
3. Proceed as for Blender Wheat Cakes, page 110.

Blender Barley Oat Cakes

Wheat is not essential to light, fluffy pancakes. Rather, some of the sweeter and more cakelike combinations eliminate wheat altogether. Barley and oats produce a golden cake reminiscent of refined flour, but with the full and satisfying flavor of whole grains.

1/3 c. oat groats
1/3 c. whole hulless barley
1 c. water
2 whole eggs
3 T. cold pressed safflower oil
1/4 tsp. sea salt
1 tsp. lecithin granules
1 T. raw unfiltered honey
1/2 c. powdered instant non-fat milk
1 1/2 tsp. baking powder

1. Pre-soak the oats and barley in water.
2. In the morning, proceed as for Blender Wheat Cakes, page 110.

Blender Soy Cakes

Wheat combines best with the flavor of soy, which can often overpower less distinctive grains. Forget about grinding soybeans to flour. Simply pre-soak along with the wheat and let the blender take care of the batter.

These full bodied pancakes take a bit longer to cook—about 2-3 minutes on the first side and 1-2 more on the second. Full cooking is essential for soybeans, which contain an enzyme that interferes with protein assimilation unless it is cooked. Make sure the batter is thoroughly blended. You may want to process the beans and wheat at a higher speed to make sure that the soybeans are pureed.

> 1/2 c. hard wheat berries
> 1/4 c. raw dried soybeans
> 1 1/4 c. water
> 2 whole eggs
> 3 T. cold pressed safflower oil
> 1/4 tsp. sea salt
> 1 tsp. lecithin granules
> 1 T. raw unfiltered honey
> 1/2 c. powdered instant non-fat milk
> 1 1/2 tsp. baking powder

1. Pre-soak the wheat and soybeans in water.
2. In the morning, proceed as for Blender Wheat Cakes, page 110.

Blender Variations

The list of variations, substitutions and additions is potentially infinite. There are Maslin cakes (1/3 c. wheat and 1/3 c. rye), Garbanzo cakes (follow the recipe for Soy Cakes, but use garbanzo beans instead) and Almond/Wheat (1/2 c. soft wheat berries, 1/4 c. almonds) to name a few.

In devising your own recipes, keep the following basic rules in mind:

1) Different grain groups behave differently in liquid combinations.
2) Make sure that substitutions are made from the same group. Corn and rice, for example, are similar in terms of their tardiness in absorbing liquids. Finely ground rice flour would then be a fine substitute for corn flour. Whole wheat, oat groats, buckwheat groats, barley, rye and triticale all generally display the same properties. The beans, soy and garbanzo, could likewise be interchanged. Usually more water is required for bean ingredients. The nuts and seeds form a group of their own; they generally do not make up more than 1/3 of the grain/seed total, although this is not a hard and fast rule. Finally, bran and wheat germ are similar partners in the pancake world.

Once the batter is blended, there are even further variations that the breakfast cook can make. These come in the form of additions, which can include 2-3 T. of dried shredded coconut, chopped raw or roasted seeds or nuts, roasted peanuts, or roasted soybeans. These should be stirred into the batter by hand and not blended, since texture as well as nutritional value is the goal.

Do not hesitate to experiment. Remember that whole grains vary in their moisture absorbing properties, depending upon grain type and storage conditions. So if the batter is too thick, add a tablespoon or two of water; if it is too thin, sprinkle in some bran or wheat germ until the desired consistency is reached. Next time you make pancakes, remember to adjust the water measure.

Yeast Pancakes

Why yeast pancakes? There are several reasons. Yeast raised pancakes have a different texture from those using baking powder. Yeast pancakes trap the gases formed by growing and multiplying yeasts within the gluten network of the batter. Since wheat has more gluten than any other grain, it is necessary to maintain at least 1/2 cup of whole wheat flour in each batch of yeast pancakes. Best results are achieved using 3/4 cup hard wheat flour and making quarter cup substitutions of other flours or nutrition boosters.

Yeast pancakes that have to be started the night before or in the earliest hours of morning somehow never seem to get made. The rule in our house has always been a limit of one hour of preparation for breakfast. If it can't be made in an hour's time, it isn't on the menu. For this reason, the basic yeast recipe is one that will produce light, nutritious pancakes, within 60 minutes of measuring the ingredients.

Nutritionally, yeast pancakes differ from baking powder pancakes and crepes. Because of the yeast structure, the batter requires less egg—only 1 for whole wheat pancakes and none for buckwheat. However, the action of the yeast on the grain frees up important minerals that might otherwise be bound up in insoluble compounds and therefore be unavailable to the body.

Buckwheat, not being a true grain, does not behave like other cereal grain flours. It can hold its rise by a gelatinous network which is formed when liquid is beaten into the ground kernel. Sprouting buckwheat, with its black husk, can be used, but the finest, lightest pancakes will be obtained by grinding the shelled groats into flour.

Whole Wheat Yeast Pancakes

1 c. lukewarm water*
1 T. dry active yeast
1 T. raw unfiltered honey
1 T. cold pressed corn oil
1 c. hard wheat flour
1/4 tsp. sea salt
1 tsp. lecithin granules
1/3 c. powdered instant non-fat milk
1 whole egg

1. In a medium bowl, measure the water. Add the yeast, honey and oil. Stir. Let the yeast proof for ten minutes. At the end of this period it should be foamy.
2. While the yeast is dissolving, measure into a small bowl the flour, salt, lecithin and milk.
3. Beat the egg into the yeast with a whisk.
4. Stir in the dry ingredients for one minute, using a whisk and stirring in rapid circular strokes. Cover with a dish or towel and let the batter rise in a warm place until light—anywhere between forty minutes and one hour, depending upon the temperature of the kitchen or warming oven. The oven in a gas range with a pilot light is ideal. So also is the warming oven of a wood cookstove. If your kitchen is unusually cool, you can use a pre-warmed electric heating pad.
5. A half hour before the end of this rising period, heat the griddle and make sure it is well seasoned. The batter for yeast pancakes has less oil and may tend to stick more than the batter for baking powder pancakes. (A larger quantity of oil makes the pancakes heavier.)
6. Stir down the batter, which should have doubled in volume, and spoon or ladle onto a medium hot griddle. Bake 1 1/2 to 2 minutes on the first side, until the tops are bubbled and the sides are dry. Turn, cook another 1 1/2 minutes and serve. The pancakes will be about 1/4 inch thick.
7. Serve them with butter and maple syrup or fruit sauce and yogurt.

Serves 2 (twelve 4 inch pancakes)

Optional

Add 1/4 tsp. cinnamon to the batter.

* Water that feels neither hot nor cold when dropped on the wrist.

Wheat Germ Yeast Pancakes

1. Into a one cup measure, spoon 1/4 cup wheat germ (raw). Fill to one cup level with whole wheat flour (hard). Proceed as for Whole Wheat Yeast Pancakes, using the wheat germ/wheat mixture in place of 1 cup hard wheat flour.

These are nutritionally superior to regular yeast cakes, providing 18 g. protein per serving.

Whole Grain Variations

Hard wheat flour with its high gluten content works up into the ideal batter for yeast cakes. However, other whole grain flours—oat, triticale, or rye—can be substituted in amounts up to 1/3 cup for an equal amount of hard wheat flour. Soft wheat flours, such as white wheat and pastry wheat will yield a softer crumb and can be substituted for the full amount of hard wheat flour (one cup).

Soy flour has a strong taste. It has no gluten at all (since beans are legumes) providing no framework for the yeast-producing gases. When adding soy flour, use only 1/4 cup in place of an equal measure of hard wheat flour.

Buckwheat Cakes

For buckwheat enthusiasts—a modern version of an early American standby. Traditionally, buckwheat cakes call for baking soda dissolved in water to be added to the batter before baking. This procedure, which is also standard for many sourdough recipes, lightens the pancakes. The extra soda may not be desirable, however. In this recipe, the yeast does it all. Buckwheat dominates the flavor, while part wheat flour improves the texture.

If desired, these cakes could be made with 100% buckwheat flour. An egg would also increase the protein. If adding the egg, beat it into the dissolved yeast, reducing the lukewarm water to 1 cup.

> 1 1/4 c. lukewarm water
> 1 T. dry active yeast
> 1 T. molasses
> 1/2 c. powdered instant non-fat milk
> 2/3 c. buckwheat flour
> 1/3 c. hard wheat flour
> 1/4 tsp. salt
> 1 tsp. lecithin granules

1. In a medium bowl, measure the water, yeast, molasses and milk. Let the yeast proof. It should get foamy.
2. While the yeast is dissolving, combine the buckwheat and wheat flour, the salt and lecithin in a small bowl. Beat the flour mixture into the foaming yeast and let rise for 45-50 minutes, or until light.
3. Stir down and spoon onto a medium hot griddle. Bake slowly, watching to see that the bottoms do not brown too quickly. Turn when the sides are browned and the tops bubbled.

Serve with butter and maple syrup. The traditional accompaniment is a molasses and butter sauce.

IV

Yeast
and
Other Early Risers

There is a kernel of truth to the old adage that man does not live by bread alone, but with a little forethought and the combination of complementary proteins, the breakfast cook can at least get the day off to a good start with yeasted rolls and egg rich muffins. These doughs and batters (so called because of the yeast in the dough and baking powder or baking soda in batter) require different cooking times, ranging from quick muffins to yeast muffins to whole wheat dough.

This chapter is not intended to teach the basics of bread making. Instead I have emphasized a high protein, basic, whole wheat dough that can be made up into interesting rolls and buns that will tempt the breakfast-shy members of the family while making sure that they are getting approximately 10 grams of protein per two small rolls, muffins or buns. Whole wheat flour by itself cannot supply enough protein to meet that one-third of the day's requirement at breakfast time unless one were to consume over a cup of flour (in which case the calorie content alone would be prohibitive). Yet when whole wheat joins with other grains, eggs, milk and protein boosters, the combination yields a high energy breakfast food that provides protein, fiber and minerals. By filling the dough with cheese, ground nuts, seeds, or a combination of these, the protein content of each roll goes up even higher.

Rolls or muffins made from the basic doughs and batters should always be accompanied by a glass of milk or a serving of yogurt or yogurt nog to complete the protein requirement (at least 20 grams). Milk is a wholesome food, rich in calcium, and the liberal use of it is encouraged.

However, for those unable to ingest milk, nut or seed spreads in place of butter will boost the breakfast protein. Some of the filled rolls will supply adequate protein in a two roll serving without the addition of anything more.

Basic Whole Wheat Yeast Dough

_____ Bread, Rolls and English Muffins _____

At last, 100% whole wheat yeast dough with a bounce—moist, light rolls and buns that can be cut, rolled, twisted and filled to any-one's preference.

— Mixing the Dough —

1/2 c. lukewarm water
2 T. dry active yeast
1 tsp. raw unfiltered honey
1 c. water
1/3 c. powdered instant non-fat milk
1/3 c. raw unfiltered honey
1/2 c. cold pressed safflower oil
2/3 tsp. sea salt
2 eggs
2 T. lecithin granules
5 c. whole wheat flour (hard wheat)

1. In a small bowl, measure and stir the water, yeast and honey. Let stand 10 minutes while preparing the other ingredients. At the end of the 10 minutes, the yeast will be foamy, so be sure that the bowl is not too small.
2. Warm, in a medium stainless bowl until the honey is dissolved, the water, milk, honey, oil and salt.
3. In a separate small bowl, beat the eggs. Add them to the yeast.
4. Combine the two liquids.
5. Stir the flour/lecithin into the liquid ingredients using circular strokes until thoroughly combined. Cover and let rest 30 minutes.

— Two Methods of Raising and Kneading —

There are two methods of raising and kneading, for differing temperaments. The first is for those who enjoy the physical activity and rhythm of kneading; the second is for those who know they will never last the 10 minutes of rocking and rolling the dough.

Take your choice:

I. Ten full minutes of kneading develops strong bands of gluten that contribute to a springy roll.

1. After the 30 minute rest, scrape the dough onto a well-floured surface (wooden board or formica counter top) and knead for ten minutes. Watch the clock and make sure you give the dough the full measure of kneading. Let this be a time of enjoyment, with thoughts of the good food you are preparing or the interesting projects you have planned, and the time will pass quickly.
2. Oil the original mixing bowl. Return the dough ball to the bowl and invert so that the complete dough surface is coated with oil.
3. Cover and let rise in a warm location (preferably a warming oven or high up in the house—remember, heat rises). It should be double in approximately one hour. A finger poked into properly risen dough will leave its imprint.
4. Punch down the dough and let rise again, covered, for another 45 minutes.
5. Punch down again at the end of this second rising and turn the dough onto the kneading surface. Cover with a tea towel and let rest for 10 minutes while oiling or buttering 2 large cookie sheets.
6. Roll and shape according to preference.

II.
1. With lightly oiled hands, punch down the dough after the 30 minute rest. It will be sticky, but the oil will keep your hands clean of the dough. Freshly ground whole wheat needs time to absorb moisture from the liquid ingredients. This method, by delaying the kneading, gives the wheat extra time to utilize existing moisture. Consequently, less additional flour is necessary when it comes time to knead.
2. Let the dough rise, covered, another half hour, then punch down again.

3. Repeat. This will take 90 minutes in all from the time the dough was stirred.

4. Turn the dough onto a lightly floured board or table top (formica) and knead 3-5 minutes. Be sure to scrape the bowl clean.

5. Oil the bowl, return the dough to it, then invert the ball so that it is completely covered with a thin layer of oil.

6. Cover and let rise until double—around 40 minutes.

7. Punch it down, turn onto a board (no additional flour will be necessary), cover and let rest for 10 minutes.

8. Oil or butter 2 stainless cookie sheets while the dough is resting.

9. Roll out and shape according to preference.

—Shaping the Dough—

Rolls

One recipe makes 24 rolls. Two rolls made from the basic whole wheat dough recipe provide approximately 9 grams of protein and can be shaped as cut buns, crescents, clover leaves, or round rolls.

1. **Cut Buns.** Simply cut the dough up into 24 pieces with a serrated knife and place them, evenly spaced on one large buttered cookie tray (approximately 14 x 16 inches) or two small, round, buttered cake pans (8 inches in diameter).

2. **Crescents** can be formed by cutting the dough into thirds, rolling each third into a circle 1/4 inch thick, then cutting the circular dough into 8 triangular pieces, as for pie. Roll each wedge from the base of the triangle to the apex, curving the roll into a crescent as you place it on the cookie tray.

3. **Clover Leaves** take a bit more time to shape, but make an attractive alternate to crescents. Cut, as for cut buns, then pinch each piece of dough into three smaller pieces. Form each of these small thirds into round balls and place in buttered muffin tins.

4. **Round Rolls** are formed simply by cutting as for cut buns and shaping each dough piece into a round ball and flattening slightly with the palm of the hand as it is placed on the buttered cookie tray.

Baking time for rolls is 20-25 minutes, 350 degrees F. Remove from trays immediately and let cool on wire racks.

English Muffins

Roll the dough out 1/2 inch thick, then cut out with a 3 inch ring (a cleaned, empty 8 oz. ring pineapple can or 6 oz. tuna can is ideal). Place the rounds on a corn meal sprinkled surface and let rise, covered, for about 20 minutes, or until doubled. Bake slowly on a seasoned griddle for 6-7 minutes on each side. Eat warm or cool thoroughly, split with a fork, and serve toasted with butter, nut butters or peanut-honey spread.

Loaves of Bread

Basic whole wheat dough, with or without additions, can be shaped into loaves, 3 small loaves 7 3/8 x 3 5/8 x 2 1/4 inches or two larger loaves. The smaller loaves allow you to divide the dough in thirds and experiment with three different fillings.

Baking time for small loaves is 45-50 minutes, 350 degrees F. For large loaves, 50-60 minutes, 350 degrees F.

—Additions to Basic Dough—

The basic dough can be made higher in protein by the substitution of high protein flours or the addition of ground nuts, seeds, or grated cheese.

1. After stirring in the whole wheat flour/lecithin, stir in 1 c. raw hulled sunflower seeds. This will add 35 g. of protein per recipe, which translates into an additional 3 g. of protein per 2 roll serving.
2. Stir in 1 1/2 c. shredded cheddar cheese after the whole wheat flour/lecithin addition. This 42.5 g. protein bonus means over 3.5 g. more protein per 2 roll serving.
3. Stir in 1/2 c. roasted peanut flour (made by grinding roasted Spanish peanuts in the blender), 1/2 c. almond meal or 1/2 cup cashew meal (made in the blender or electric grinder) for an extra gram of protein in each morning's serving.
4. For cinnamon raisin rolls, add 1 tsp. cinnamon to the flour, and stir 1/2 c. snipped raisins and 1/2 c. sunflower seeds into the dough after the flour addition for an extra 1.5 grams of protein per serving plus all the minerals of raisins, particularly iron and calcium.

—Substitutions—

1. In place of 5 c. whole wheat flour, use 4 2/3 c. whole wheat flour and 1/2 c. full fat soy flour. Proceed as for Basic Whole Wheat Dough. Soy adds .5 g. protein per serving.
2. In place of 5 c. whole wheat flour, use 4 2/3 c. whole wheat flour and 1/2 c. raw wheat germ. Proceed as for Basic Whole Wheat Dough. Wheat germ adds .5 g. protein per serving.

Amounts larger than 1/2 cup of soy or wheat germ will significantly alter the flavor of the rolls. Experiment, using your own taste buds. Just keep the total flour at approximately 5 cups, slightly more for non-cereal substitutions. Be sure to use hard wheat for your flour, since its higher protein means higher gluten. The softer wheats will not hold the escaping gases from the yeast which make for a light loaf.

Basic Whole Wheat Dough can also become rye, oat, buckwheat, triticale, barley or corn dough by substituting up to 1 cup of any of these flours (or a combination of them) for the same amount of whole wheat flour in the original recipe. Instead of honey, try sorghum or molasses with the stronger flavored flours, such as rye or buckwheat.

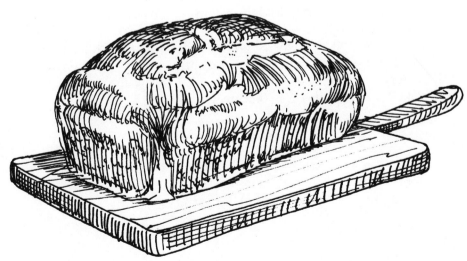

Fillings for Loaves and Rolls

There are three basic approaches to filled bread: 1) the loaf (German stollen, Polish poppy seed rings and Slavic potica); 2) Kolaches, which center the filling in an envelope of dough; 3) filled rolls, or snails, which are a cut version of the filled loaf. For each of the three varieties, divide the Basic Dough recipe, page 125, into three parts and work one section at a time. You may want to increase the honey in the Basic Whole Wheat Dough to 1/2 cup.

Stollen

1/3 recipe Basic Whole Wheat Dough
1/2 c. dried fruits, diced
    any combination desired: pineapple, papaya,
    apricots, golden raisins, etc.
1/4 c. apricot juice
1/2 c. raw almonds

1. Place the fruit and juice in a small saucepan. Heat until juice is absorbed. Set aside.
2. Chop the almonds coarsely.
3. With 1/3 of the roll dough (page 125), pat out or roll a rectangle approximately 16 x 5 inches.
4. Spread with the fruit mixture, then sprinkle with almonds.
5. Roll lengthwise. Then fold the roll over on itself and twist it in the shape of a cruller.
6. Put the twist in an oiled or buttered 7 3/8 x 3 5/8 inch loaf pan or on a buttered cookie sheet. Let rise until double—approximately 30 minutes.
7. Bake for 45 minutes at 350 degrees F.

This recipe yields 1 small loaf.

Almond Potica

1/3 recipe Basic Whole Wheat Dough
1 c. raw almonds, finely chopped
2 T. raw unfiltered honey
1/4 tsp. vanilla
2-3 drops almond flavoring (extract)
1/4 tsp. cinnamon
1 beaten egg
several T. double milk, see page 4

1. Combine, in a small bowl, the almonds, honey, vanilla, almond extract, cinnamon and egg.
2. Add enough double milk (by the tablespoon) to make the mixture of a spreadable consistency.
3. Spread the mix on a 16 x 6 inch rectangle of dough, page 125-127, and roll widthwise. The Potica will have concentric circles when cut or you may roll lengthwise and double the roll over on itself and twist. The latter method will distribute the almond filling throughout the dough.
4. Place the roll or twist in a buttered loaf pan (7 3/8 x 3 5/8 inches) or on a buttered cookie sheet and let rise until double, approximately 30 minutes.
5. Bake for 45 minutes at 350 degrees F.

Maple Pecan Roll

1/3 recipe Basic Whole Wheat Dough, page 125
1 c. coarsely chopped raw pecans
1/4 c. pure maple syrup

1. Simmer the pecans and maple syrup until the syrup turns cloudy and begins to foam. This will not take more than 5 minutes. Cool. The maple syrup will thicken as it cools.
2. Prepare the dough the same as for stollen. Spread the maple pecan mixture evenly over the rectangle and roll up from the narrower (or width) end of the rectangle.
3. Place in a buttered loaf pan (7 3/8 x 3 5/8 inches) or a buttered cookie sheet. Let rise until double (about 30 minutes).
4. Bake for 45 minutes at 350 degrees F.

Sunflower Potica

1/3 recipe Basic Whole Wheat Dough, page 125
1 c. raw hulled sunflower seeds, ground
1/4 c. raw unfiltered honey
1/2 tsp. vanilla
1 beaten egg

1. Prepare the dough as for Almond Potica, page 131.
2. Combine the other ingredients.
3. Add enough double milk, see page 4, a tablespoon at a time, to make a spreadable consistency.
4. Proceed as for Almond Potica.

Cut Filled Rolls or Snails

To make almond, sunflower, or maple pecan rolls, simply roll the above loaves widthwise and slice each into 8 rolls. Place the rounds in a buttered 8 x 8 inch pan and let rise until double—20-30 minutes. Bake for 25 minutes at 350 degrees F.

Cheese goes well with almonds and complements the protein. To boost the protein of the almond rolls, sprinkle 1 cup grated cheddar cheese over the almond filling mixture before rolling, then roll and cut into 8 snails. Let rise until double and bake 25 minutes at 350 degrees F.

Sesame Apple Snails

1/3 Recipe Basic Whole Wheat Dough, page 125
2 c. chopped raw apple, cored
1/3 c. raw unfiltered honey
1/4 tsp. cinnamon
1/2 c. toasted sesame seeds

1. Combine the apple, honey and cinnamon in a saucepan. Bring to a boil and simmer for 5 minutes. Cool.
2. Spread the apple mixture on a dough rectangle. Sprinkle with sesame seeds.
3. Roll and cut.
4. Transfer the rounds to a buttered 8 x 8 inch baking pan.
5. Let rise until doubled in bulk (approximately 20 minutes).
6. Bake at 350 degrees F. for 25 minutes.

Cheddar Apple Rolls

Prepare the apple filling for Sesame Apple Snails, page 133. Sprinkle 1 cup grated cheddar cheese on the spread apple filling. Then roll and slice into 8 rounds. Place these rounds in a buttered 8 x 8 inch baking pan. Let rise until double. Bake for 25 minutes at 350 degrees F.

Kolaches

Divide the Basic Whole Wheat Dough or any of its variations into thirds. Roll each third into a rectangle approximately 12 x 6 inches. Cut each rectangle into 8 squares and place 2 level tablespoons of any of the cut roll or snail fillings in the center of each square. Join the opposite ends of each square at the center, over the filling, to form an envelope of dough. Transfer each "wrapped" bun to a buttered baking pan or buttered stainless cookie sheet. Let rise until double (20-30 minutes) and bake for 25 minutes at 350 degrees F.

Stewed dried fruits also make excellent kolache fillings. Any dried fruits can be used. Simply simmer the fruit in a minimum of water until the fruit is soft and the liquid is evaporated. The idea is to steam the fruit rather than boil it—the dough will not be able to hold the filling if there is any excess liquid.

Sweeten the fruit with honey to taste, then cool. Brands such as Timber Crest require no further sweetening.

Use 2 tablespoons of cooked fruit filling to the bun.

Stewed fruit fillings do not add significantly to the protein content of the breakfast. You should therefore serve these kolaches with a glass of milk or an additional prepared egg to make the morning's protein requirement.

Muffins

Muffins, honey sweet and hot from the oven, are always a breakfast treat. They are one of the most versatile of breakfast foods. Fruits, spices, nuts are all welcome additions to the basic batter.

Muffins are a solution for wheat-allergic or milk-allergic breakfasters. The entire range of flours—oat, barley, rice, corn, triticale, rye and buckwheat—can be substituted whole or in part for the wheat flour in the basic recipe. Milk solids may be omitted and fruit juice substituted for the water. Or, omit the milk solids and use soy or nut milk in place of the water. (For a delightful change, keep the milk solids in the recipe, but use the nut milk in place of the water.) Even eggs are unnecessary. Eggless muffins have a good rise and produce a more cakelike product with a pleasing texture. To prove that nothing is sacred to the muffin, you can leave out the baking powder/baking soda and use yeast for leavening. In each case, the end result will be a delightfully scented fresh morning bread.

Two muffins are usually considered a serving when accompanied by a glass of milk, a small dish of yogurt, or an egg or two (a glass of yogurt nog would do it all!). One batch of 12 muffins makes enough for several breakfasts.

Serve the muffins hot out of the oven. After the muffins have cooled, leftover muffins can be frozen either in aluminum foil (shiny side in) or in airtight plastic bags. If you use aluminum foil, you can save one step and reheat them, still enclosed in foil, in the oven. If you use plastic bags, remove the muffins from the bags, place the muffins in aluminum foil and heat in a 350 degrees F. oven 20 minutes.

Should you find yourself with week old muffins, turn them into bread pudding.

Hard wheat flour requires more liquid than soft (white or pastry) wheat. When you are experimenting on your own, always be sure to use 1 cup of liquid for hard wheat or part hard wheat, and 3/4 cup of liquid for soft wheat and all other flours or flour combinations.

The way you mix the batter is of prime importance. Ironically, the more hastily you mix, the better the muffin. Use a wooden spoon, not a whisk, and start stirring in broad strokes the moment after you pour the liquid ingredients into the dry. The object is to combine, not blend—a whisk does more than is required—to the detriment of the texture. Forget about circular strokes; stir crosswise, around, and crosswise again. By the time you have counted to 10, all dry ingredients should be moistened and the batter will be ready to pour or spoon into the muffin tins. Sometimes, depending upon the protein and moisture content of the grain, it will be easier to spoon the batter into the muffin cups rather than pour it. However, if the batter appears thin, simply pour it from the bowl, using a rubber spatula to cut off the flow of batter between muffins. Oil can be used in place of butter in the muffin cups, but proves more troublesome when it comes time to remove the muffins from the pan.

High oven heat is essential for proper texture. A muffin should be uniformly crowned (not wobbly peaked or flat). Unless the oven is at 400 degrees F. when the muffin tin goes in, no number of good intentions or well stirred batters will produce the right muffin. When properly mixed and baked, the muffin will be spongy and light, and will break without crumbing. And it will appear to be tunnelled with air pockets. Muffins made without eggs will not be so tunnelled. They will have the appearance of cake.

Graham Muffins
(Basic)

2 c. whole wheat flour (hard wheat)
1/4 tsp. sea salt
1 T. lecithin granules
1 tsp. baking powder (Rumford's)
1/2 tsp. baking soda
1/4 c. cold pressed safflower oil
1/4 c. raw unfiltered honey
2 eggs
1/3 c. powdered instant non-fat milk
1 cup water (room temperature)

1. Preheat oven to 400 degrees F.
2. Measure into a medium bowl and combine the flour, salt, lecithin, baking powder and soda.
3. In a small bowl, measure and whisk together the oil, honey, eggs, milk and water.
4. Pour the liquid ingredients into the dry all at once. Then stir quickly, using broad strokes to moisten the dry ingredients. Do not beat or use a whisk. The batter should not be smooth, like cake batter. You should use a minimum of strokes.
5. Hard wheat makes a stiffer batter than pastry wheat. The resulting batter should be spooned into buttered muffin tins. Using a large serving spoon, measure 2 spoonsful into each muffin cup. As a general rule, the muffin tins should be between 1/2 and 2/3 full.

   Bake the muffins in a 400 degree F. oven for 20 minutes. If the oven is working properly, there is no need to peek, since opening the oven door only means the muffins may collapse. Allow the muffins to cool 5 minutes after baking. Then remove them from the muffin tin and transfer to a plate or dish, setting the muffins on their sides instead of bottoms. This prevents moisture from building up at the bottoms of the muffins, making them soggy. Cover the muffins with a tea towel until ready to serve. Serve with butter, fruit purees or nut butter spreads.

High Energy Graham Muffin Variations

For increased protein, the basic mix can be altered to include soy flour or wheat germ as part of the dry component.

Graham/Wheat Germ Muffins

Use 1 3/4 cups graham flour and 1/4 cup wheat germ in place of 2 cups graham flour. Yield: 12 muffins. The muffins will be 4.7 g. protein per muffin.

Graham/Soy Muffins

Use 1 3/4 cups graham flour and 1/4 cup full fat soy flour in place of 2 cups graham flour. Yield: 12 muffins. Each muffin contains 4.7 g. protein.

Pastry Muffin
(Basic)

More like cake than muffins. This recipe is an excellent way to introduce your family to whole wheat.

2 c, whole wheat pastry flour
1/4 tsp. sea salt
1 T. lecithin granules
1 tsp. Rumford's baking powder
1/2 tsp. baking soda
1/4 c. cold pressed safflower oil
1/4 c. raw unfiltered honey
2 eggs
1/3 c. powdered instant non-fat milk
3/4 c. water (room temperature)

1. Preheat oven to 400 degrees F.
2. Measure into a medium bowl and combine the flour, salt, lecithin, baking powder and soda.
3. Measure into a small bowl and whisk together until smooth the oil, honey, eggs, milk and water.
4. Pour the liquid ingredients into the dry all at once. Then combine with broad strokes, using a wooden spoon. Stir across the bowl as well as around, making sure that all dry ingredients on the bottom of the bowl are moistened.
5. Pour the batter into a buttered muffin tin with 12 cups, filling each one slightly more than half full.
6. Place the muffin tin in the center of the oven and bake for 20 minutes at 400 degrees F. without opening the oven door.
7. Remove from the oven and let cool for 5 minutes. Remove muffins from the tin and transfer them to a plate. Place the blade of a dinner knife straight down the side of each muffin to pry it loose from the tin. If it does not pop out right away, run the knife around the entire muffin and gently lever it out. Place the muffins on their sides on the plate. This allows the air to circulate and prevents moisture (from escaping steam) to build up on the bottoms of the muffins. Cover with a tea towel.
8. Serve warm with butter, fruit purees or nut butter spreads.
Yield: 12 muffins.

High Energy Variations

Pastry/Wheat Germ Muffins

Use 1 3/4 c. whole wheat pastry flour and 1/4 c. raw wheat germ in place of 2 c. whole wheat pastry flour.

Pastry/Soy Muffins

Use 1 3/4 c. whole wheat pastry flour plus 1/4 c. full fat soy flour in place of 2 c. whole wheat pastry flour.

Wheatless Muffins

Flours from grains other than wheat make delicious muffins. Grind the grain fine and follow the recipe for Basic Pastry Muffins. Combine different flours in any proportions you choose. The following descriptions serve only as a guide to get you started.

The fun of making muffins is really in the mixing of flours, and you can come up with your own hybrid muffin by combining different flours to total 2 cups. Flour combinations also boost the nutritional power of the muffins, since complementary proteins are made available to the body at the same time.

100% Barley Muffins

These are mild flavored muffins that take well to spices and chopped apples (fresh or evaporated). Try adding 1 tsp. cinnamon and 1/2 c. chopped apples (evaporated; use 1 c. fresh) to the batter or a combination of apples and dates.

100% Buckwheat Muffins

Grind buckwheat groats to a fine powder (the hulls of sprouting buckwheat are too tough to use) and sweeten with molasses instead of honey for a change. A fine grained muffin, distinctively flavored, with an affinity for spiced fruit butters or purees.

100% Corn Muffins

For those who enjoy the pure flavor of corn: grind yellow or white field corn to a fine flour and use in place of wheat flour in the Basic Muffin recipe. This fragrant muffin proves that corn does not always require wheat to make a perfect muffin.

100% Oat Muffins

Grind whole oat groats or rolled oats to a fine powder. The muffins are delicate and fine grained, like sponge cakes. Their natural sweetness combines well with coconut. Try dusting the buttered muffin tins with dried shredded coconut before pouring in the muffin batter. Oat flour takes well to all spicing.

100% Rice Muffins

They are sweet, moist and chewy, more like dessert than breakfast. Use short or long grain brown rice, and grind it as fine as possible in a (Corona) steel mill.

100% Triticale Muffins

Triticale makes a good hearty muffin—more dense than muffins made from other non-wheat flours. It has a taste all its own, like neither of its parents. This hybrid of wheat and rye does the mixing of grains all by itself.

Specialty Muffins

These recipes require adjustments in the proportion of the ingredients and are listed separately for that reason. If substitutions are made, be sure they are comparable. Use oat or barley flour in place of whole wheat pastry flour, since barley and oat most closely resemble soft wheat in texture and moisture absorbing properties. They are also mild flavored. For more protein, soy or wheat germ can always be substituted for part of the flour component—usually in the proportion of 2 tablespoons per cup. This amount will not affect the flavor of the muffin.

Carob Muffins

For plain carob flavor, serve these with butter and honey. For devoted peanut butter fans, carob/peanut spread is a must. To boost the protein of these muffins, add 1/2 c. chopped or ground almonds, cashews or walnuts to the batter after it has been stirred.

1 1/2 c. whole wheat pastry flour
1/2 c. carob flour
1 tsp. cinnamon
1 T. lecithin granules
1/4 tsp. salt
1 tsp. baking powder
1/2 tsp. baking soda
1/4 c. raw unfiltered honey
1/2 c. cold pressed safflower oil
2 eggs
3/4 c. water (room temperature)
1/3 c. powdered instant non-fat milk
3 T. dried shredded coconut (optional)
1/2 c. chopped raw almonds, cashews or walnuts (optional)

1. Preheat oven to 400 degrees F.
2. In a medium bowl, measure and combine pastry flour, carob, cinnamon, lecithin, salt, baking powder and soda.
3. In a small bowl, whisk until smooth the honey, oil, eggs, water and milk.
4. Pour the liquid ingredients into the dry and stir briskly. (See directions for Basic Pastry Muffins.) At this time, either or both of the following optional additions may be stirred in: 3 T. dried, shredded coconut and 1/2 c. chopped raw almonds, cashews or walnuts.

Bake as for Basic Muffins.

Yield: 12 muffins

Maple Pecan Muffins

2 c. whole wheat pastry flour (or high energy substitute)
1 T. lecithin granules
1/4 tsp. sea salt
1 1/2 tsp. baking powder
1/4 c. pure maple syrup
1/4 c. cold pressed safflower oil
2 eggs
3/4 c. water (room temperature)
1/3 c. powdered instant non-fat milk
1/2 tsp. vanilla
1/2 c. chopped raw pecans

1. Into a medium bowl, measure and combine the flour, lecithin, salt and baking powder.
2. In a small bowl, whisk until smooth the maple syrup, oil, eggs, water, milk and vanilla.
3. Pour the liquid ingredients into the dry and stir quickly. (See instructions for Basic Pastry Muffins).
4. Stir in the pecans.
5. Pour or spoon into buttered muffin tins.
6. Bake 20 minutes at 400 degrees F.
Yield: 12 muffins

Sesame Cheese Muffins

One cup of grated (shredded) cheese adds 28 grams of protein to the batter. Add sesame seeds to that and you have an especially delicious as well as nutritious muffin.

Prepare batter for Basic Graham Muffins, page 137, or Basic Pastry Muffins, page 139, reducing the honey to 2 tablespoons.

Have ready 1 c. shredded cheddar cheese and 1/4 c. toasted unhulled sesame seeds (see About Roasting Nuts). Stir the cheese and nuts into the combined batter. Spoon into buttered muffin cups that have been dusted with finely grated Parmesan cheese. Bake 20 minutes at 400 degrees F. Be sure to serve warm; the cheese hardens upon cooling.

Yield: 12 muffins

Peanut Butter Muffins

These rise high, filling the kitchen with the aroma of fresh roasted peanuts.

dry ingredients Basic Graham, page 137,
   or Basic Pastry Muffins, page 139
1/2 c. creamy natural (or homemade) peanut butter
2 T. cold pressed safflower oil or peanut oil
1/4 c. raw unfiltered honey
2 eggs
3/4 c. water (room temperature)
1/3 c. powdered instant non-fat milk
1/2 c. chopped roasted peanuts, with skins

1. Preheat oven to 400 degrees F.
2. Measure the dry ingredients for Basic Graham or Basic Pastry Muffins or any flour variation of these two.
3. In a small bowl, whisk together the peanut butter, oil, honey, eggs, water and milk.
4. Pour the liquid ingredients into the dry and stir quickly, until just combined.
5. Add the chopped peanuts.
6. Spoon into buttered muffin cups and bake 20 minutes at 400 degrees F.
Yield: 12 muffins

Corn Muffins

100 % corn muffins are delicious in their own right, but they do not provide the protein quantity or quality of this recipe, which combines complementary proteins.

> 1 c. corn flour*
> 3/4 c. whole wheat pastry flour
> 1/4 c. soy flour
> 1/4 tsp. sea salt
> 1 T. lecithin granules
> 2 tsp. baking powder
> 1/4 c. cold pressed safflower oil
> 1/4 c. raw unfiltered honey
> 2 eggs
> 3/4 c. water (room temperature)
> 1/3 c. powdered instant non-fat milk
> (1 c. shredded cheddar cheese)

1. Preheat oven to 400 degrees F.
2. Into a medium bowl, measure and combine the corn, wheat and soy flour, the salt, lecithin and baking powder. If you do not wish to use soy flour, add 1/4 cup white pastry flour, making 1 cup in all.
3. In a small bowl, whisk until smooth the oil, honey, eggs, water and milk.
4. Pour the liquid ingredients into the dry and stir briskly.
5. At this time, if desired, add the cheese.
6. Spoon or pour the batter into buttered muffin cups and bake 20 minutes at 400 degrees F.
Yield: 12 muffins

* Corn flour is whole corn ground to a fine powder just as you would grind wheat.

Wheat Germ Muffins

Yogurt makes a more tender crumb in these muffins, but regular milk solids and water can also be used. For adjusting recipes, follow these basic rules:

1) When using all pastry wheat or other non-wheat flour combinations, use 1 c. yogurt in place of 3/4 c. water and 1/3 c. milk solids. Use 1 1/2 tsp. baking soda in place of the baking powder/soda combination in the Basic Muffin recipe.

2) When using all hard wheat or part hard wheat, use 1 1/4 c. yogurt and 1 1/2 tsp. baking soda in place of the baking powder plus soda.

3) Use yogurt whey instead of water, but do add the 1/3 c. milk solids. Replace the baking powder plus soda with 1 1/2 tsp. baking soda.

4) You may find that when using yogurt or whey, you will want to increase the honey to 1/3 cup.

 1 1/2 c. whole wheat pastry flour
 1/2 c. raw wheat germ
 1/4 tsp. sea salt
 1 T. lecithin granules
 1 1/2 tsp. baking soda
 2 eggs
 1/3 c. raw unfiltered honey
 1 c. plain yogurt
 1/4 c. cold pressed safflower oil

1. Into a medium bowl, measure and combine the flour, wheat germ, salt, lecithin and baking soda.
2. Into a small bowl, whisk together until smooth the eggs, honey, yogurt and oil.
3. Pour the liquid ingredients into the dry.
4. Combine and bake as for Basic Muffins.

Mix or Match Grain Flakes Muffins

Oat, wheat, barley, rye or triticale flakes make flavorful muffins with an interesting, chewy texture. A soft wheat flour makes a moist springy matrix for the flakes, but matching flours can also be used in place of wheat. For example, a 100% oat muffin can be made by using oat flakes and oat flour. The same applies for the other flakes.

Grain flakes vary in thickness and occasionally wheat flakes will be quite thick. If this is the case, use boiling water for the soaking and let the flakes soak for up to an hour. You can check every 15 minutes to see how they are softening.

Mix and match. The following is a guide only, so feel free to substitute any flake or flour.

Oat Flake Muffins

The milk is double rich in this recipe, to boost the protein of each muffin to 5 grams.

> 1 c. rolled oats
> 1 c. water plus 2/3 c. powdered instant non-fat milk
> 1 c. whole wheat pastry flour*
> 1/4 tsp. sea salt
> 1 T. lecithin granules
> 1 tsp. baking powder
> 1/2 tsp. baking soda
> 2 T. cold pressed safflower oil
> 1/4 c. raw unfiltered honey
> 2 eggs

1. Soak the oats in water and milk for 15 minutes or until softened.
2. Preheat oven to 400 degrees F.
3. Measure into a medium bowl and combine the flour, salt, lecithin, baking powder and baking soda.
4. In a small bowl, whisk together the oil, honey and eggs.
5. Add the soaked oats to the liquid ingredients.
6. Pour the mixture into the dry ingredients and mix and bake as for Basic Muffins.

---

* Increase the water to 1 1/4 c. if using hard wheat flour.

Bran Muffins

Each muffin supplies 1 tablespoon of vital bran fiber.

1 1/4 c. hard wheat flour (graham)
3/4 c. miller's bran
2 tsp. baking powder
1/4 tsp. sea salt
1 T. lecithin granules
2 T. raw unfiltered honey plus 2 T. molasses
   Or 1/4 c. sorghum
2 eggs
1 c. water
1/3 c. powdered instant non-fat milk
2 T. cold pressed safflower oil
1/2 c. snipped raisins or dates
1/4 c. raw hulled sunflower seeds

1. Preheat oven to 400 degrees F.
2. Into a medium bowl, measure and combine the flour, bran, baking powder, salt and lecithin.
3. In a small bowl, whisk together until smooth the sweetener, eggs, water, milk and oil.
4. Pour the liquid ingredients into the dry and stir briskly.
5. Add the raisins or dates and sunflower seeds.
6. Bake as for Basic Graham Muffins.

Soft wheat flour or oat flour take best to subtle flavorings, while graham flour works best with more dominant flavors, such as cinnamon and molasses.

Spice Muffins

This is a lightly spiced muffin.

any basic muffin recipe, page 137 or 139
1 tsp. cinnamon
1/4 tsp. allspice
dash nutmeg
1/2 c. snipped raisins, dates, figs, or prunes
1/2 c. raw hulled sunflower seeds

1. Add cinnamon, allspice and nutmeg to the dry ingredients of any basic muffin recipe.
2. After the batter has been stirred, add the dried fruit and sunflower seeds.
3. Proceed as in Basic Recipe.

If you have trouble with the fruit or nut additions sinking, toss them lightly with pastry flour before stirring them into the batter.

Spiced Rye Muffins

Spicing is more pronounced in these deliciously scented muffins, since it is designed to complement 100% rye flour. However, the combination of spices works well with graham or triticale flour, too.

basic muffin recipe
1/2 tsp. cinnamon
1/4 tsp. powdered cloves
1/4 tsp. allspice
1/8 tsp. cardamon
1 tsp. orange zest
1/2 c. snipped raisins

1. To the dry ingredients, add the spices and orange zest.
2. To the stirred batter, add the raisins.
3. Proceed according to Basic Recipe.

Date Nut Muffins

basic muffin recipe
1/2 tsp. cinnamon
1/2 c. chopped pitted dates
1/2 c. coarsely chopped walnuts or cashews
   OR
   1/2 c. raw hulled sunflower seeds

1. To the dry ingredients of any basic muffin recipe add the cinnamon.
2. After the batter has been stirred, add the dates and walnuts (or cashews or sunflower seeds).
3. Proceed according to directions in Basic Recipe.

Gingerbread Muffins

any basic muffin recipe
1 tsp. cinnamon
1 tsp. ginger
1/4 c. molasses
2 T. honey
1/2 c. raw hulled sunflower seeds or chopped raw cashews
1/2 c. snipped raisins

1. Add the cinnamon and ginger to the dry ingredients.
2. For sweetening, use the molasses and honey.
3. To the stirred batter, add the sunflower seeds or cashews and the raisins.
4. Proceed according to recipe.

Coconut Almond Muffins

any basic muffin recipe
1/3 c. honey
1/2 tsp. each vanilla and almond extract
1/2 c. dried shredded coconut
1/2 c finely chopped or ground raw almonds

1. Increase the honey in any Basic Muffin Recipe to 1/3 cup.
2. Add to the liquid ingredients the vanilla and almond extracts.
3. To the stirred batter, add the coconut and almonds.
4. Proceed according to recipe.

Crumb Cake Muffins

Crumb toppings turn regular breakfast muffins into holiday fare. Make up any muffin batter, pour it into buttered muffin cups, then sprinkle the following crumb topping over the batter in each cup. The crumbs will appear to be sinking, but will rise to the top and brown perfectly, provided the oven has been preheated and you bake the muffins immediately.

Crumbs for 12 muffins:
>   1/2 c. rolled oats
>   1/3 c. graham flour
>   3 T. dried shredded coconut
>   2 T. cold pressed safflower oil
>   2 T. raw unfiltered honey

1. In a small bowl, measure the oats, flour and coconut.
2. In a measuring cup, emulsify with a fork the oil and honey.
3. Pour the honey/oil over the dry ingredients and mix with a fork until all the dry ingredients are uniformly coated and the mixture forms small crumbs.
3. Sprinkle on top of each muffin before baking.

Dried Fruit Nut Muffins

Dried fruits vary in moisture content and you will have to proceed accordingly. Fruits that have been sulfured generally do not require pre-soaking and can be added directly to the batter. The same is true of Timber Crest's "Sonoma" pack, which is a moisturized dried fruit. Regular bulk pack dried fruits, however, will require a pre-soak period so that they do not rob the muffins of moisture. If the fruit is extremely leathery, presoak it by covering the chopped fruit with boiling water about an hour before baking or the night before you plan to make muffins. Drain the fruit and use the reserved juice as part of the water measurement. This can be done in one easy procedure: drain the fruit by holding a strainer over a one cup measure, then add enough water to reach the required level.

To make fruit and nut muffins, add to the stirred batter (any Basic Muffin Recipe) 1/2 cup of any combination of diced, dried fruit: apricots, pears, peaches, light raisins, pineapple and papaya. Also add 1/2 cup of any combination of chopped raw nuts: cashews, pecans and walnuts. Incorporate the dried fruits and nuts into the batter quickly.

Berry Muffins

Fold 1 cup fresh or frozen berries in Basic Pastry Muffins or 100% Oat Muffins. You may want to incrase the honey to 1/3 cup.

Fruit Juice Muffins

Fruit juice can be substituted for water and milk solids in any basic muffin recipe. When using naturally sweet juices, such as apple, orange or pineapple, reduce the honey to 2 T. For Graham Muffins, use 1 cup of fruit juice; for Pastry Muffins, use 3/4 cup fruit juice.

When using fruit nectars, such as apricot, peach, or pear, use 1 1/4 cup of nectar for Graham Muffins, 1 cup for Pastry Muffins.

If milk allergy is not a problem, powdered milk can be added along with the fruit juice. One-third cup of instant powdered non-fat milk adds 10 grams of protein to the batter and mellows the flavor of the fruit.

Cinnamon Apple Muffins

1. To the dry ingredients of any muffin recipe, add 1 tsp. cinnamon.
2. For liquid ingredients, substitute pure unsweetened apple juice for water.
3. Omit milk solids.
4. Reduce honey to 2 T.
5. To the stirred batter, add 1/2 c. chopped evaporated apples and 1/2 c. chopped walnuts or cashews.

Eggless Muffins

Make sure to grind the grain to a fine flour and proceed with any muffin recipe, with the following change: increase the water by 1/3 cup for hard wheat, and 1/4 cup for soft wheat. Without eggs, the flavor of the grain is more pronounced.

Yeast Muffins

This is the solution for those who would prefer not to use baking powder or baking soda for leavening yet still want a rise. A yeast muffin is somewhere between a muffin and a bread, and makes a nice change of pace as an accompaniment to breakfast eggs or yogurt. It is light and less sweet than a Basic Muffin and goes well with butter, honey, honeyed fruit purees or peanut/honey spread. Cheeses also go well with yeasted muffins. The wheat flour is necessarily dominant, since at least 2/3 of the flour component must be wheat flour in order to supply the yeast gases with enough gluten to expand the dough. The only exception to this rule is buckwheat, which can be used in place of hard wheat.

Yeast Muffin

1 c. lukewarm water
1/3 c. powdered instant non-fat milk
2 T. cold pressed safflower oil
2 T. raw unfiltered honey
1/2 tsp. sea salt
1 T. dry active yeast
2 beaten eggs
1 T. lecithin granules
2 c. hard wheat flour (graham)

1. Combine in a medium bowl the water, milk, oil, honey, salt and yeast. Let the yeast proof, about 10 minutes.
2. Add, stirring vigorously, the eggs, lecithin and flour.
3. Cover and let rise until doubled, about 1 hour.
4. Stir down the batter, then spoon it into buttered muffin pans.
5. Let the muffins rise until doubled (they will crest their individual cups). This will take about 25-30 minutes.
6. Sprinkle the tops with any of these: raw unhulled sesame seeds or poppy seeds or chia seeds.
7. Bake 25 minutes in a 375 degree F. oven. Remove from the muffin tin immediately and let cool on a wire rack. If the muffins stick to the pans, run a blunt knife around the muffin tin and lever the muffin out.

Yeasted Muffin Variations

Add to the above batter (after it has risen, but before spooning it into the buttered muffin tins) any of the following:
1) 1 tsp. cinnamon, 1/2 c. snipped raisins and 1/2 c. raw hulled sunflower seeds
2) 1/4 c. toasted unhulled sesame seeds and 1 cup shredded cheddar cheese
3) 1/2 c. chopped roasted peanuts

Possible Flour Mixtures for Yeasted Muffins

Combine 1 2/3 cup graham flour and 1/3 cup of any of the following: oat flour, rye flour, barley flour, buckwheat flour (made from groats), corn flour, triticale flour, rice flour (from brown rice). You may also combine any of the flours for the 1/3 cup measurement.

Eggless Yeasted Muffins

They will rise as well as muffins with eggs but are lower in protein. Be sure to add cheese or nuts to the batter if you omit the eggs.

Follow the recipe for The Yeast Muffin but increase the water to 1 1/4 cups.

Extra Hints for Extra Protein

1) To any muffin recipe, add nuts or cheese.
2) Substitute soy flour or raw wheat germ for part of the regular flour.
3) Dust the buttered muffin cups with raw wheat germ and/or sprinkle the tops of the muffins with raw wheat germ before baking.
4) Dust the buttered muffin cups with ground nuts or seeds and/or top the unbaked muffins with more ground nuts or seeds.
5) Dust the buttered muffin cups with grated Parmesan cheese.

V

Accompaniments

*Custards, Sauces,
Spreads and Toppings*

Custards

Custards are so called because they rely upon eggs to thicken the milk mixture, while puddings use arrowroot or cornstarch to make them set. Custards may be prepared in the morning within the hour and served warm. Or they may be prepared the night before and served chilled. These egg-rich recipes are especially high in protein, but eggs and milk alone do not provide fiber. To meet the morning's requirement for fiber, they should be served with a topping of any of the following: granola, High Fiber Crunchy Wheat Germ, peanuts, carob, coconut, any chopped nuts or seeds.

Honey is specified as the sweetener in the custard recipes, but maple syrup or part maple syrup and/or sorghum and molasses also produce fine textured custards. The stronger flavored syrups, such as molasses and sorghum, are more valuable from the standpoint of mineral content, but since their flavor dominates the custard, their inclusion is a matter of personal preference.

For variety, try almond flavoring in place of vanilla with carob and coconut flavors.

Baked Custard
(Basic)

This low fat recipe will make a four serving bowl of custard that supplies 13.5 g. of protein per serving.

4 eggs
1/4 c. raw unfiltered honey
1 tsp. lecithin granules
2 c. water (room temperature)
1 c. powdered instant non-fat milk
(1/8 tsp. sea salt)
1/2 tsp. vanilla
pinch nutmeg

1. Preheat oven to 325 degrees F.
2. In a medium bowl, beat the eggs.
3. Beat in the honey, lecithin, water, milk, salt and vanilla.
4. Pour the mixture into an ungreased 1 qt. glass baking dish, and sprinkle with nutmeg.
5. Place the glass dish in a pan of hot water and set the pan in a 325 degree F. oven. The pan of hot water insures a smooth texture. (Custard left to its own devices in the oven may toughen). Bake for 40-50 minutes or until set. A knife inserted an inch from the edge of the custard will come out clean if the custard is done baking.
6. Cool slightly and serve warm (or chilled) with granola, crunchy wheat germ and/or fruit sauce.

Variations
1) Substitute unsweetened fruit juice for water in the Basic Baked Custard recipe. Milk solids may or may not be included. When using apple juice, sprinkle the custard with cinnamon instead of nutmeg.
2) **Carob Custard:** One quarter cup of carob sauce (see page 198) stirred into the Basic Baked Custard Recipe before baking produces a 2 layered custard, "regular" custard on top and carob custard on the bottom, which tastes like Swiss milk chocolate.
3) **Peanut Butter Custard:** This is a lightly flavored custard; feel free to add more peanut butter to suit individual tastes. The peanut butter rises to the top, combining with egg and milk to make a peanut sponge layer on top of the regular custard. Simply add 1/4 c. peanut butter spread to the Basic Custard Recipe, stirring it into the beaten eggs.
4) **Coconut Custard:** Add, to the unbaked Basic Custard, 1/2 c. dried shredded unsweetened coconut.

Rice Custard

A high fiber (rice bran) custard that is equally rich in protein, zinc, calcium, potassium and iron.

> **Basic Baked Custard recipe**
> 2 c. cooked brown rice
> 1/4 c. chopped pitted dates
> 1/4 c. coarsely chopped walnuts, cashews or
>   whole hulled sunflower seeds
> pinch cinnamon

1. Before baking, stir into the Basic Baked Custard the rice, dates and walnuts (or cashews or sunflower seeds).
2. Sprinkle with cinnamon and bake the custard at 350 degrees F. in a 1 1/2 qt. glass baking dish that has been set in a pan of hot water. Check the custard after 45 minutes with a knife to see if it is set.

Variations
1) Use 1/4 c. pure maple syrup in place of honey.
2) Serve with raspberry glaze.
3) Garnish with honey toasted wheat germ, toasted coconut, chopped dry roasted almonds or chopped roasted peanuts.

COOKED BROWN RICE

One half cup raw brown rice is the equivalent of 2 c. cooked rice. Bring 1 1/4 c. water plus 1/8 tsp. salt to a boil. Pour in 1/2 c. raw brown rice. Do not stir. Resume boil, cover and simmer 1/2 hour. Remove from heat and let steam an additional 10 minutes. Use hot or cold for rice custard.

Stove-Top Rice Cream Custard

Eggs and milk cooked on top of the stove require more attention, but produce a creamier custard that is more like pudding.

2 c. cooked brown rice
4 eggs
1 tsp. lecithin granules
1/4 c. raw unfiltered honey
2/3 c. powdered instant non-fat milk
1 1/3 c. water (room temperature)
1/2 tsp. pure vanilla
1/4 c. chopped pitted dates
1/4 c. coarsely chopped walnuts or
    raw hulled sunflower seeds (whole)

1. In a medium saucepan, whisk together the rice, eggs, lecithin, honey, milk and water.
2. Cook over medium low heat, stirring constantly, until the mixture thickens. When it coats a wooden stirring spoon, it is done. This usually takes around 10 minutes.
3. Stir in the vanilla, dates and walnuts, or sunflower seeds.
4. Transfer to a 1 1/2 qt. glass serving dish or individual bowls (four 10 oz. bowls) and serve warm or chilled, with or without fruit sauce.

Wheat Berry Cream Custard

This is another breakfast custard that provides its own fiber. Substitute 2 cups cooked whole wheat berries for rice in the stove-top rice recipe. The "cream" thickens upon cooling. Vary the flavor by mixing in dried apples or raisins with the chopped dates.

Variations
1) For a firmer custard, follow the Baked Rice Custard recipe, substituting the cooked berries for brown rice.
2) Substitute cooked whole oat groats, triticale or barley for the wheat berries, or make a mixture of these grains. (This is a perfect use for leftover whole berry cereal.)

Crumb Custard

Eggs, milk and whole grains—it's all there in one dish. This is truly a custard, although bread or cake crumbs baked in an egg/milk matrix are classically called puddings.

    4 muffins
       OR
    4 basic whole wheat rolls
    2 c. water
    1 c. powdered instant non-fat milk
    4 eggs
    1 tsp. lecithin granules
    1/4 c. raw unfiltered honey
    1/2 tsp. vanilla
    1/4 tsp. cinnamon
    1/4 c. raisins
    1/4 c. raw hulled sunflower seeds

1. Dice or crumb 4 muffins or 4 rolls and place in a buttered 1 1/2 qt. glass baking dish.
2. Mix the water and milk. Pour over the muffins or rolls.
3. Beat together the eggs, lecithin, honey, vanilla and cinnamon. Pour over the soaked crumbs and toss lightly with a fork.
4. Toss in the raisins and sunflower seeds.
5. Place the crumb custard dish in a baking pan filled with approximately 1 inch of hot water and place in a 350 degree F. oven for 45 mintes. Insert a knife near the edge of the bowl to see if the custard is done.
6. Serve warm or chilled with yogurt or double milk, page 4.

Variations
1) Add 1/2 c. dried shredded unsweetened coconut to the crumbed bread or muffins.
2) Swirl 1/3 c. carob sauce (see page 198) into the mixed custard just before baking.

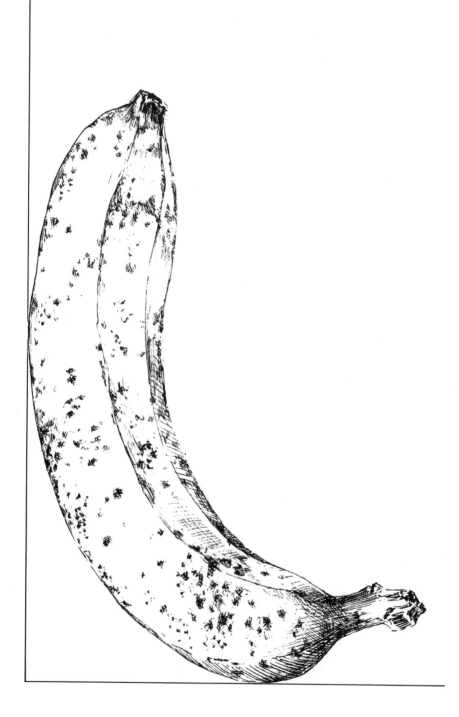

Yogurt

Yogurt is a living food, and should be eaten with its health sustaining organisms (any combination of *lactobacillus bulgaricus, streptococcus thermophilus* and *lactobacillus acidophilus*) intact. For this reason, few cooked recipes in this book call for yogurt. Rather, it should be eaten as a topping or as a base, then piled high with fruits, nuts, wheat germ and/or granola.

The bacteria which reside in a healthy intestine are capable of producing the B vitamins and vitamin K. The activity of these valuable organisms, which can also destroy other undesirable and harmful bacteria in the intestinal tract, is enhanced by the ingestion of yogurt or *acidophilus* (*acidophilus* will not in itself turn milk to yogurt, but is usually added to the yogurt culture).[1] Therefore, yogurt is an essential breakfast food for those who wish to start the day off right. Persons who have difficulty digesting regular pasteurized milk may find yogurt tolerable, since the milk protein is already broken down by the culture organisms by the time it appears on the breakfast table.

There is a great deal of controversy at present over the contaminant level in fresh cow's milk. Much of what the cow ingests in concentrated in the milk fat. It is possible that the process of homogenization destroys most of the milk's vitamin A.[2] Powdered whole milk is equally suspect because of nutrient deterioration over long term storage. There is also evidence pointing to the destruction of the amino acid lysine when milk is canned or dried, which would include both whole and skim milks.[3]

The following low-fat recipe is a compromise, devised to maximize protein and minimize the dangers lurking in much of the fresh milk now available on supermarket shelves.

---

[1] Adelle Davis, *Let's Get Well*, pp. 144-146.

[2] Adelle Davis, *Let's Eat Right to Keep Fit*, p. 58.

[3] *Ibid.*, p. 37.

Low Fat Yogurt

This is similar to the Adelle Davis recipe, though it was concocted by three Alaskan women living 500 miles from fresh milk. In its original form, it was incubated in a water bath on top of an Ashley wood stove.

One cup of Low Fat Yogurt provides 12 grams of protein, a considerable protein boost when compared to commercially available yogurt, which averages 8 to 10 grams per cup.

There are several types of "starters" or cultures that can be used: 1) 3 tablespoons of plain yogurt, from your own previous batch or a friend's, 2) 10 g. dried yogurt culture, available in health food stores. Some dried yogurt packets come in 5 g. sizes. You can make a full batch with this small quantity, but it will take longer for the yogurt bacteria to multiply and set the milk. 3) Three yogurt capsules, each supplying in excess of 20 million *lactobacilli*. These capsules, containing freeze dried yogurt, are commercially prepared by vitamin companies to be swallowed by persons who do not care for yogurt or who cannot tolerate eating it. They make an inexpensive starter for yogurt, an important factor since the culture must be renewed about once a month. The capsules also store well. To use the capsules, pull apart the gelatin shells and sprinkle the powder over the warmed milk mixture. Stir the powder into the milk, then add the empty gelatin shells. These will dissolve as the yogurt sets.

> 1 pkg. unflavored gelatin (1 T.)
> 1/2 c. cold water
> 4 cups boiling water
> 2 c. powdered instant non-fat milk
> 1 can (13 oz.) evaporated milk
> 1 c. more water, hot or cold
> dried yogurt culture or 3 yogurt capsules
> 3 T. plain yogurt

1. In a medium bowl dissolve the gelatin in cold water. This is done by sprinkling the gelatin over the water and letting it absorb water for about 10 minutes.
2. Add the boiling water.
3. Whisk in the dried milk and the evaporated milk.

4. Take a reading with a yogurt thermometer (or regular thermometer with low temperature readings). The milk mixture must be around 110 degrees F. before the yogurt culture can be added.

5. Add 1 c. more water, either hot or cold, to heat or cool the mixture to around 110 degrees F.

6. If using dried culture, stir it into the milk mixture at this point. If using yogurt from a previous batch, mix it and a few T. of warm milk in a small bowl. Stir until smooth, then pour it back into the milk mixture. Mix well.

7. Yogurt can be made in a 2 qt. stainless or Corning ware bowl, or individual glass dishes, whichever you prefer. If you use a large container, the yogurt can be mixed directly in it, then covered, since contact with light destroys the vitamin B2 in milk. If you don't have a yogurt maker to incubate the milk mixture, the dish (or dishes) should be put in a warm water bath and incubated for approximately 5 hours at a temperature around 110 degrees F. Put an immersible thermometer in the water so that you can check it easily. I use a roasting pan as an incubator, and put in enough water to bring the water level to 1/2 inch from the top of the yogurt dish. Drape a dish towel or two over the covered yogurt bowl and pan of water to avoid drafts and keep in the heat. Set the bowl in a warm place: a gas oven with a pilot light, the warming oven of a wood cook stove, or a heating pad are fine. Electric fry pans set on low heat have also been converted into successful water bath incubators; just be sure to set the yogurt bowl on a rack so that the bottom is not in direct contact with the pan.

Yogurt will be loosely "set" when done. If it is not set, incubate it another hour or more until it definitely gels, then refrigerate immediately to stop the action of the yogurt bacteria. Overincubation will result in sour, watery yogurt. Set the finished yogurt in the refrigerator for at least 10 hours (less for smaller batches or dishes of yogurt) before eating. It needs the chilling and rest to set up firmly and keep its even texture.

Fresh Milk Yogurt

If you have a good source of pasteurized whole milk, there is no equal to it in terms of the yogurt texture. Fresh milk makes a thick, creamy yogurt that surpasses the best sour cream.

With the addition of 1/2 c. powdered instant non-fat milk which thickens the yogurt and bolsters it nutritionally, each cup of this fresh milk yogurt will supply 11.5 g. protein, in addition to calcium, phosphorus, vitamins B1, B2 and B6.

> **4 c. whole fresh milk**
> **1/2 c. powdered instant non-fat milk**
> **3 T. plain yogurt**

1. In a saucepan, scald* the milk.
2. Stir in the dried milk.
3. Cool the milk to 110 degrees F. Cooling time can be hastened by placing the saucepan in a sink or pan full of cold water and stirring. Stirring exposes as much milk as possible to the cooled sides of the pan. When the temperature has reached 110 F., remove the pan from the cold water bath.
4. Measure the yogurt and thin with several T. of warm milk.
5. Stir the thinned starter into the warmed milk mixture and incubate as for Low Fat Yogurt.

---

* The definition of scalding varies from cookbook to thermometer, spanning temperatures from 150 degrees F. to 212 degrees F. Technically, milk is scalded when it is brought almost to a boil, but not allowed to roll at 212 degrees F.

Why scald? The original purpose of scalding milk was to destroy bacteria. All raw milk should still be scalded. Pre-heating to the boiling point also affects the milk's ability to set, thus hastening the yogurt process and improving the texture of the yogurt. For this reason, even pasteurized milks are still scalded for yogurt. Yogurt made from powdered and canned evaporated milks, however, eliminate the scalding stage since the milks have already been subjected to heat.

Sweetened Yogurt

True yogurt devotees will enjoy the flavor of yogurt unadulterated. Others may only indulge when the tartness is mollified. For yogurts that will be eaten in the morning, only a minimal amount of sweetening should be added. Too much sugar, whether it comes in the form of fruit or honey, can cause an alkaline reaction in the stomach and interfere with calcium absorption.

Two tablespoons of maple syrup can be stirred directly into the yogurt. Raw unfiltered honey can also be used to soften the tang of the yogurt, but it tends to solidify as it stands. If it is more solid than liquid, briefly warm it and measure into the dish in which the yogurt will be mixed. When it has cooled to room temperature, add a small amount of plain yogurt and stir until the honey is dissolved (or uniformly distributed throughout the yogurt). Then stir in the rest of the plain yogurt.

Keep in mind that stirring breaks down the culture matrix and will make the yogurt more like a thick cream sauce.

Flavored Yogurt

Yogurt can also be sweetened with dried fruit purees, honey sweetened jams and marmalades, or fresh mashed or pureed fruits. These sweeteners impart their flavors as well as their sugars to the yogurt.

As a general rule, use 2 T. fruit puree or jam or 1/4 c. fruit sauce for each cup of yogurt. Please adjust for personal preference.

The fruits can be mixed with the yogurt so that their flavor is evenly distributed. Or the fruit can be layered alternately with the yogurt (sweetened or not) in a glass dish. A stemmed goblet makes an especially attractive serving dish for yogurt swirls. Try alternate layers of yogurt, mashed banana and date spread for an exotic treat.

Other variations include Carob Swirl and Peanut Butter Yogurt. To make a Carob Yogurt Swirl, alternate layers of sweetened yogurt and carob sauce (page 198) in a glass dish. Garnish with Carob Granola (page (page 35).

For Peanut Butter Yogurt, mix equal parts of sweetened yogurt and Peanut Butter Sauce (page 197). If you do not have Peanut Butter Sauce prepared, combine 2 T. natural peanut butter and 2 tsp. to 1 T. raw unfiltered honey. Fold in 1/2 c. plain yogurt slowly. Serve garnished with chopped roasted peanuts, Peanut Cashew Granola or Crunch, Toasted Wheat Germ. You may want to layer the Peanut Butter Yogurt with thin slices of ripe banana.

Breakfast Yogurt

Plain, sweetened or flavored yogurts become true breakfast foods when topped with the extra protein and minerals of wheat germ, nuts, seeds, fruit and lecithin. Topping mixtures can be combined to meet special dietary needs and/or allergies. Oat based granolas, for example, can take the place of wheat germ for those who are allergic to wheat.

Fill a cereal bowl with your favorite yogurt (1 cup minimum) and top with at least 1/4 c. crunchy wheat germ (Regular or High Fiber), 2 T. sunflower seeds or chopped nuts, 1 tsp. lecithin granules, any fruit, fresh, stewed or dried, which has been mashed, sliced or diced, a drizzle of maple syrup (optional).

The Crunchy Wheat Germ combinations in Chapter II (pages 40-44) will turn a bowl of yogurt into a delicious breakfast. Granolas are a ready made addition to the breakfast yogurt bowl. Since the volume/protein ratio differs, increase the measure of granola to 1/2 cup when using it instead of wheat germ.

Think about these flavor combinations: bananas go well with chopped roasted peanuts or cashews. Raisins and sunflower seeds go well together. Also pineapple chunks and dried shredded coconut. The combinations are infinitely exciting.

Yogurt Nog

Yogurt Nog is an extremely versatile drink that supplies 14 g. of protein when made with Low Fat Yogurt and extra large eggs. Additions such as wheat germ or nuts or higher protein concentration than the almonds called for in Traditional Nog can increase the nutritional yield. The flavor of yogurt nog can be altered in a variety of ways, depending upon the additions. Frothy peanut or carob drinks can be made by the addition of natural peanut butter (1/4 c. to the basic recipe) or carob powder. Or try them both together! Fresh and dried fruits also make refreshing drinks when added to cool yogurt and whipped to a foamy nog. The basic recipe takes on new dimensions with each variation. Make a date shake by substituting 1/4 c. dates for the honey or try an orange egg cream by whipping 1/4 c. orange concentrate into the nog. Sweetness and taste are individual matters—for some, 1/4 c. of orange concentrate will take the place of honey, while for others, the drink will taste right with the concentrate added to the basic nog recipe (with honey).

A nog is naturally thick. For holiday breakfasts, blend in a ripe banana and/or fold whipped cream or whipped chilled evaporated milk into the basic nog, then top with grated nutmeg. Whipped cream provides very little protein, but is rich in vitamin A, with smaller amounts of calcium, phosphorus and potassium. Evaporated milk, on the other hand, is rich in all the milk minerals as well as being high in protein. Be sure it is thoroughly chilled before beating (24 hours in the refrigerator or until crystals form around the edges when placed in a bowl in the freezer.)

Another way of making a super thick yogurt nog is to separate the eggs, blending only the yolks with the other ingredients. Beat the whites to stiff peaks in a separate bowl. Slowly fold a small amount of the blended yogurt into the whites with a rubber spatula. Then steadily add more blended yogurt until the two are uniformly combined. Beating the whites increases the volume of the drink considerably, so be sure to use large enough glasses. One recipe still makes 2 drinks. Yogurt nog prepared in this way is like a milk shake. It can be served at the time of preparation or chilled before serving. Place the nog in the freezer for a short time. If you cool it in a refrigerator, it may separate.

Some people cannot tolerate raw egg because a substance in the white, avidin, will combine with biotin, a B vitamin, in such a way that the body cannot absorb the biotin, thus creating a deficiency. If this is a problem, eggs can be left out of the nog.

Molasses and sorghum are alternate sweeteners for yogurt nogs, although they result in drinks that differ considerably from the traditional egg nog. Molasses is strong enough to mask the flavors of torula and brewers yeast, both of which are excellent nutrition boosters.

Basic or Traditional Nog

Grind a cupful or more of nuts ahead of time and store, covered, in the refrigerator. The small quantities called for in yogurt drinks can then be readily measured. This recipe serves 2.

2 eggs
1 c. plain low-fat yogurt
2 T. honey or maple syrup
1 tsp. lecithin granules
1/4 tsp. vanilla
2 T. ground almonds or cashews
pinch nutmeg

1. In a blender, measure the eggs, yogurt, sweetener, lecithin, vanilla and nuts.
2. Frappe, pour, sprinkle with nutmeg and serve.

Variations

Try any of the following additions to the basic recipe, adjusting the honey: 1/4 c. stewed fruit (with juice), 1 banana, 1 whole fresh fruit (pitted or cored), 1/4 c. natural peanut butter, 1/4 c. dried raisins, 1/4 c. chopped dates, sunflower seeds, sesame seeds or lightly toasted wheat germ in place of almonds or cashews, 1/4 c. cashew butter, 1/4 c. sesame butter.

Combine several of the above—1 whole banana plus 1/4 c. natural peanut butter, or the chopped dates and nuts. Use a fresh orange and 2 T. dried shredded coconut. Or blend in the orange and substitute ground toasted sesame seeds or tahini for the almond meal. The yogurt base naturally complements the protein of any nut or seed, so add as many different varieties as you enjoy. Why not cashew/almond or sesame/peanut?

Serves 2

Carob Nog

Carob nog tastes like an old fashioned malted without all the sugar of the soda fountain variety.

2 eggs
1 c. plain low fat yogurt
2 T. carob powder
1 tsp. lecithin granules
1/4 tsp. vanilla or almond flavor
2 tsp. to 2 T. honey
2 T. ground almonds, cashews or peanut butter

1. In a blender, measure the eggs, yogurt, carob, lecithin, flavoring, honey and ground nuts.
2. Frappe, pour and serve.

Berry Nog

2 eggs
1 tsp. lecithin granules
1 c. plain low fat yogurt
2 to 4 T. honey sweetened berry jelly
    OR 1/4 c. berry sauce

1. In a blender, measure the eggs, lecithin, yogurt, jelly or sauce.
2. Frappe, pour and serve.

The amount of berry jelly will vary, since low methoxyl pectin*
will gel with little or no honey added to the fruit juice. Home made
jellies tend to be less sweet than those that are commercially prepared.
Try the lesser amount first to see where your jelly lies on the sweetness scale, and adjust the recipe accordingly.

Fresh berries and honey would be a fine substitute for the berry
jelly when available. Add as much as you like.

---

*See page 196.

Yogurt Custard Cream

This thick custard insures a creamy egg nog in the old time tradition while serving up a cooked egg white.

1/2 c. custard (see Rice Cream, page 167
1/2 c. plain yogurt
1 T. ground almonds
pinch nutmeg

1. Prepare the custard for Rice cream (omit the rice). Chill.
2. Blend the custard, yogurt and almonds. If you are making breakfast for two people double the recipe.
3. Serve in chilled glasses, sprinkled with nutmeg.

OR, use the following recipe, which makes enough custard for 2 drinks. Double, triple, and so forth as needed. To save on time and energy, make a large batch, keep refrigerated and use over several days.

2 eggs
2 T. raw unfiltered honey
1 tsp. lecithin granules
1 c. water
1/2 c. powdered instant non-fat milk
1/2 tsp. vanilla
1 c. plain yogurt
2 T. ground almonds
pinch nutmeg

1. In the top of a double boiler, whisk together the eggs, honey, lecithin, water and milk.
2. Heat the water in the bottom of the double boiler and continue to whisk or stir custard until thickened. Remove from heat and stir in the vanilla.
3. Chill.
4. Blend with the yogurt and ground almonds.
5. Serve at once with a sprinkling of nutmeg, if desired.
Any of the variations, including Carob (page 180) will turn this holiday drink into a beverage for all seasons.

Eggless Yogurt Nog

A wide assortment of eggless yogurt drinks can be prepared using the same additions as for Basic Yogurt Nog. To replace the frothiness of the beaten egg, be sure to use a plain yogurt that has been made with gelatin, such as Low Fat Yogurt. There is no reason why you could not prepare Fresh Milk Yogurt with gelatin for the purpose of whipping it up into thick drinks. Simply dissolve 2 tsp. plain gelatin in 2 T. cold water and add it to the hot milk before culturing. (This produces an exceptionally creamy yogurt as well as a thick drink.) You may even find that you will want to increase the gelatin in the Low Fat recipe as well. The addition of instant non-fat milk powder makes the eggless nog protein-rich and creamy. Depending on the gelatin content of the yogurt (some commercial yogurts are extremely high in gelatin, which enables the producer to list a higher protein content than the milk alone would warrant), you may want to thin the drink with water or fruit juice. This will not be necessary with home made yogurts, however.

Two servings of eggless yogurt nog provide approximately 14.5 grams of protein each.

1 c. plain yogurt
1 T. honey
1 tsp. lecithin granules
1/4 tsp. vanilla or almond flavoring
1/2 c. powdered instant non-fat milk
2 T. ground almonds or cashews
(2-4 T. water or fruit juice)

1. In a blender, measure the yogurt, honey, lecithin, flavoring, dried milk and nuts. If necessary, add water or fruit juice to thin the drink to the desired consistency.
2. Frappe, pour, and serve. Any of the **Variations** additions, page 179, will further thicken the drink.

Sauces, Spreads and Toppings

To achieve the goals of breakfast cooking, good taste and nutrition, one should take full advantage of the healthful benefits and eye appeal afforded by sauces, spreads and toppings. These "extra" items, which can turn an ordinary stack of pancakes into a gourmet breakfast, may actually form the nutritional backbone of the meal.

Sauces can be made from fruits, nuts, carob or a combination of these. Fruits are particularly valuable in terms of minerals, and should appear with each breakfast to insure an adequate supply of potassium. The body requires potassium to balance sodium and chlorine (the two elements of salt, NaCl). At other meals, vegetables provide large quantities of potassium. At breakfast, this requirement is usually fulfilled by fruit. Calories alone limit the quantity of fruit one might wish to serve with the morning meal. The suggested portions that follow were devised with a view to maintaining body weight given a moderately active schedule. Fruit sugars, while they are naturally occurring sweeteners, still put on pounds when the body does not have the opportunity to use up those sugars as fuel.

Ground nuts or whole seeds can be added to any fruit sauce to supply extra protein and interesting texture. For full nut flavor, use nut butter (made from roasted nuts) as a base for sauce. Use the Peanut Butter Sauce as a basic recipe and substitute other nut butters, such as almond, sesame or cashew. Date chunks and chopped roasted nuts are delicious additions. Likewise, do not hesitate to garnish a carob sauced line of rolled Swedish pancakes or crepes with chopped roasted peanuts or toasted sesame seeds.

In keeping with the first maxim of this cookbook—to eat simply— the recipes for spreads could not be easier to prepare. They are, intentionally, the most basic means of converting fruits, nuts and carob into spreadable delicacies. They are pure, wholesome and delicious. Remember, it is the combination of many simple things that turns plain fare into festive food. A simple peach spread held in the cradle of a delicate crepe, drizzled with pure maple syrup, topped with a dollop of fresh yogurt, then garnished with chopped, lightly roasted cashews and crunchy wheat germ sounds like a holiday breakfast, but you can prepare it each morning with ease.

Yogurt can be considered a topping. As such, it adds extra protein, but more importantly, it complements the protein of whole grain flours, nuts and seeds. A small swirl of yogurt on top of pancakes increases the protein value of the stack. (A yogurt nog served with a morning muffin or roll functions in the same way.)

Wheat germ is another valuable topping, which, like chopped nuts or whole seeds, contributes to the total protein content of the breakfast. Freshly toasted, wheat germ goes well on top of hot porridges. Use it liberally as a garnish on top of yogurt or other foods. Sprinkle it on just before serving so that it is crunchy when eaten.

Granola can also double as a garnish: on stewed fruit, yogurt, as the last word after the fruit sauce has been spooned over the pancakes. It is a good source of fiber as well as a protein booster. Use granola flavors that complement or contrast the base; Banana/Date Granola will enhance the flavor of banana yogurt, while Carob or Peanut Cashew Granola will provide contrasting temptations.

The secret to sumptuous breakfasts is not WHAT sauce you use, but HOW you use it. It is in the composition, the arrangement of all the healthful foods waiting to be assembled. Natural foods are marvelously simple to prepare and varied in the uses to which they may be put. The breakfast cook is their architect, building harmony, stability and strength through the elements of design.

Fresh Fruit

Fruit sauces and purees (or spreads) can be made from fruit in any form, fresh or dried. Such compotes can be highly individualized, corresponding to each person's taste preferences. Cinnamon apple may be nirvana for one person, while another will find heaven in plain mashed bananas.

The wild lingonberry and bog blueberry are two of the more prolific berries in Alaska, and we have developed a taste for their sweet/sour flavor. Fresh or frozen, these berries are never far from the pancakes. As fall gives way to winter, fresh Washington apples become available by air freight, providing a steady supply of fresh fruit through the cold months. Finally, there is rhubarb, with its powerhouse of vitamins and minerals, the one dependable source of fruit sauce at the beginning of each spring.

The recipes that follow therefore trace the course of the seasons and our diet as it conforms to the Arctic earth. Any berry will adapt to the lingonberry recipe, but less honey will be necessary due to the higher sugar content of more southern fruits. Fresh domestic fruits, such as peaches, apricots and pears, will adapt to the apple recipe.

Whole Lingonberry Sauce

This recipe can be used for chopped cranberries, huckleberries, or any other wild berry. Reduce the honey for domestic berries, such as blueberries, raspberries, strawberries or blackberries. Remember that cranberries are higher in pectin than lingonberries and will gel upon cooling without the addition of arrowroot.

1/2 c. water
1/2 c. raw unfiltered honey
1 c. washed whole lingonberries
1 T. arrowroot
1/4 c. water

1. Bring to a boil the water and honey.
2. Add the lingonberries. Simmer gently for 5 minutes.
3. Dissolve the arrowroot in water.
4. Stir the dissolved arrowroot into the sweetened lingonberries and simmer, stirring constantly, until thickened and clear.

Serve warm or cold over rolled Swedish pancakes or crepes.

Variation

To make a smoother sauce from the strained berries, first wash the berries, then place them in a saucepan with enough water to just cover them. Bring to a boil and simmer for 5 minutes. Run the berries and juice through a Foley food mill or blender so that the end result is a juice thickened with pureed lingonberry pulp. Use 1 cup of this concentrate in place of the whole lingonberries above. Dissolve the arrowroot in 2 tablespoons of water instead of 1/4 cup.

Cinnamon Apple Sauce

2 apples (washed, pared and cored, with the skins left on.
   This should make about 2 cups.)
sufficient water or apple juice for cooking the apples
1/3 c. raw unfiltered honey
1/4 tsp. cinnamon

1. Grate the apple coarsely into a medium saucepan.
2. Simmer slowly, covered, over low heat until the apples are softened.
3. Add water or apple juice, a tablespoon at a time, if the apples are dry. Fresh, juicy apples may not require any cooking liquid at all.
4. When the apples have thoroughly softened, add the honey and cinnamon. Simmer and stir for 3 minutes, so that the honey and cinnamon are well combined with the apples.
5. Serve warm or chilled.

Pineapple Sauce

1 8 oz. can of chunk, crushed, or tidbit pineapple, unsweetened
    unsweetened
additional pineapple juice to combine with fluid in can
    to make 1 c.
2 T. raw unfiltered honey
1 tsp. orange zest
2 cloves
2 tsp. arrowroot
2 T. water
(sprinkling of coconut, plain or toasted)

1. Into a 1 cup measure, drain the pineapple.
2. Add enough additional pineapple juice to equal 1 cup.
3. Transfer to a small saucepan and add the honey, orange zest and cloves. Simmer, covered, for 5 minutes.
4. Dissolve the arrowroot in water.
5. Add the dissolved arrowroot to the pineapple mixture and cook until thickened and clear. Stir in the drained pineapple.
6. Spoon over pancakes, crepes, or Swedish pancakes.
7. A sprinkling of dried shredded coconut, plain or toasted, turns the dish into a real treat.

Rhubarb Sauce

The rhubarb should marinate in the honey, so begin preparation 8-12 hours before you need the sauce.

2 c. rhubarb
1/3 c. raw unfiltered honey

1. Wash the rhubarb and dice in 1/4 inch pieces.
2. Place the rhubarb in a medium saucepan and stir in the honey. Cover and let marinate at least 8 hours.
3. Bring the mixture to a boil at the end of the marinating period, then turn off the heat.
4. Serve warm or chilled.

Dried Fruit

Dried fruits are a staple in the Alaskan diet because they can be depended upon in all seasons. There are a number of reliable organic fruit growers and large scale drying companies. (Timber Crest Farms is the largest supplier and one of the most conscientious.) Whether the dried fruit is procured from an outside source or comes from your own farm or garden, ease of storage and nutritional value make them an appealing component of the natural foods kitchen.

Dried fruits make delicious fruit sauces and purees. However, since the fruits vary in moisture content, depending on where and when they were dehydrated, only general directions can be given for making spreads and sauces.

The main attraction of fruit sauces, aside from their refreshing flavor and high mineral content, is their natural sweetness. Dates, figs and raisins, for example, do not require the addition of any further sweetener, but impart their own natural fruit sugars to the sauce. Dried apricots, peaches, pears and pineapple may need a few tablespoons of honey to bring out the full flavor of the fruit, but if the fruits have been dried at the peak of ripeness, the honey will be unnecessary. Dried pineapple obtained through Timber Crest, for example, has been saturated with pureed pineapple pulp and could not take an ounce more sweetening of any kind. It is more like sliced pineapple concentrate with double the flavor of plain pineapple. Always sample the sauce or puree without honey first and then add as your taste buds dictate.

Fruit sauces are literally mineral gold mines. One cup of apricot puree, for example, packs up to: 50 mg. calcium, 4.1 mg. iron, 75 mg. phosphorus, 780 mg. potassium, 3 mg. niacin, and 8,000 units of vitamin A. For comparison, maple syrup provides only small quantities of minerals.

To make a fruit puree or spread, which can be used on whole wheat rolls (instead of jam) or for crepes and Swedish pancakes, measure the dried fruits into a saucepan and cover them with water.

Figure 1/4 c. dried fruit per serving, and use approximately an equal amount of water as fruit. Bring the fruit and liquid to a boil, cover the pan and simmer until the fruit is thoroughly softened. Raisins may take only 15 minutes, while apricots or peaches may benefit from 30 minutes to an hour of gentle simmering. If the fruits are very dry, add more water during the cooking to keep the liquid almost level with the fruit. When the fruit is soft, remove the pan from the heat and let cool.

An alternate method for hydrating the dried fruit is to cover the fruit with boiling water (again, equal amounts of fruit and water) in the evening and allow them to stand, covered, overnight. In the morning.they will be soft enough to blend. For eating as stewed fruit, 2 to 3 additional minutes of cooking in the morning will be enough to plump the fruit.

Remove any pits from the softened fruit and transfer with the liquid to a blender approximately one cup at a time. Process at blend or puree speed for a few seconds, until the fruit and liquid have become a thickened spread.

The goal is a product the texture of a fruit butter, only you are achieving it in the reverse manner. Instead of cooking down the fresh fruit to evaporate the water, you are hydrating only enough to bring the fruit to spreadable consistency. At this point, taste to see if the puree needs additional honey and add only a tablespoon or two. Spice according to taste.

For serving on top of stack pancakes, rolled crepes or Swedish pancakes, you will want a thinner sauce that will pour over the stack and drizzle down the sides. This can be made in two ways: 1) In the blender, add water and honey, if desired, alternately to the fruit puree. Do not add more than 1 tablespoon of honey for each quarter cup of water. 2) Or you can cook the diced or chopped dried fruit in a larger quantity of water or fruit juice and then thicken with arrowroot. The following recipe will serve as a guide.

Apricot Sauce

Timber Crest dried apricots are so sweet that honey only serves to intensify the rich apricot flavor. The proportions given are for the Timber Crest label. The same company sells under three labels: Fruit pac (which is honey dipped), Sonoma (moisturized), and Timber Crest (which is quite dry and brittle).

1/2 c. dried apricot halves
1 c. boiling water
1 - 2 T. raw unfiltered honey

1. In a small saucepan, measure the apricots and boiling water. Let stand, covered, overnight.
2. In the morning, transfer the soaked apricots and juice to a blender container and process at puree.
3. Add the honey. Blend and serve.

The sauce requires no further thickening and may be warmed or reheated if desired.

This is the basic recipe to follow for sauces that have small chunks of fruit in a thickened juice. Any diced dried fruit can be substituted for the raisins. However, raisins have a high level of natural fruit sugars and may need no honey whereas other dried fruits may require the addition of 1-2 T. honey.

Raisin Sauce

Snipping the raisins releases grape sugars and fruit flavor more readily into the cooking liquid. Snip the raisins with a pair of scissors or just cut in half with a knife. Figs and prunes should be diced.

1/2 c. snipped raisins
1 c. water
1 tsp. arrowroot
2 T. water
sprinkling of cinnamon
(2 T. raw hulled sunflower seeds or chopped raw cashews)

1. Ina small saucepan, bring to a boil the raisins and water. Simmer for 5 minutes.
2. Drain the raisins, returning the liquid to the saucepan.
3. Dissolve the arrowroot in water.
4. Warm the raisin liquor and stir in the dissolved arrowroot and cinnamon.
5. Bring to a boil, stirring constantly, and simmer until the sauce is thickened and clear.
6. Add the drained raisins and the nuts, if you wish.
7. Serve warm on pancakes of all types.

FORTIFIED SAUCES _____

Fruit spreads can also be thinned to sauces with double milk, page 4, instead of water. Add approximately 1/2 cup of double milk to each cup of fruit puree. Adjust the honey to taste.

Date Spread

Dates do not require a blender but can be mashed with a fork. They make an ideal spread for any rolled pancake. The date fibers distribute evenly throughout the cooking liquid as the dates soften and eliminate the need for additional thickeners in the sauce.

1/2 c. diced or snipped pitted dates
1/2 c. water
(1/4 tsp. vanilla)

1. Place the dates and water in a small saucepan and bring to a boil, uncovered.
2. Mash the dates into the liquid with a fork. When they are completely distributed into the water, take the pan off the heat and let cool.
3. Add vanilla. Stir.
4. Serve warm or cooled on rolled pancakes.

Date Sauce

1/2 c. diced or snipped pitted dates
1 c. water
(1/2 tsp. vanilla)

1. In a saucepan, bring the dates and water to a boil.
2. Cover and simmer for 5 minutes.
3. Mash the dates with a fork. Continue to simmer while mashing. The sauce is finished when it is of uniform consistency.
4. If desired, add vanilla to the cooked sauce.
5. Serve warm over any pancake.

Fruit glazes are simply jellies that have been warmed to liquid consistency. Make your own honey-sweetened jellies from fruit juices and low methoxyl pectin, which does not require a high concentration of sugar to make jellies jell.

For each serving, warm a quarter cup of jelly over low heat, stirring until it is liquid and drizzle over selected breakfast dishes. Since glazes are generally sweeter than sauces, 1/4 cup per serving is usually adequate. Commercially prepared jellies are far sweeter than homemade jellies. 2 T. per serving will probably be adequate on these.

In the absence of a fruit gel, thicken 1/2 cup of sweetened fruit or berry juice with 1 tsp. arrowroot.

A delicate glaze best adorns a delicate pancake. Reserve these special toppings for crepes.

LOW METHOXYL PECTIN

Low methoxyl pectin is a natural pectin extracted from citrus fruit rinds. High methoxyl pectin, which is commonly used for jelly making, will set only in the presence of sugar, while low methoxyl pectin sets in the presence of calcium. Both pectin and a small amount of a calcium salt solution are added to the fruit juice to make it jell. The pectin and calcium are available from Walnut Acres in Penns Creek, Pennsylvania.

_____ Peanut Butter and Carob _____

Peanut Butter Spread

1/2 c. natural peanut butter (no oils or sugar added)
2 T. raw unfiltered honey

1. In a small bowl, combine the peanut butter and honey. Serve at room temperature as a spread for rolls, crepes or Swedish pancakes.

Peanut Butter Sauce

1/4 c. natural peanut butter
1 T. raw unfiltered honey
1/2 c. sweetened yogurt
   OR
1/2 c. double milk

1. Combine the peanut butter and honey.
2. Gradually stir in the yogurt or double milk.
3. Serve over crepes or Swedish pancakes.

Carob Sauce

It makes chocolate obsolete.

1/2 c. carob
1/2 c. raw unfiltered honey
1 c. water
1 c. powdered instant non-fat milk
2 T. lecithin granules
2 T. butter
1/2 tsp. vanilla

1. In a small saucepan, measure and combine the carob, honey, water, milk and lecithin.
2. Cook over medium heat, stirring constantly until thickened. The carob flour thickens all at once, so watch it carefully.
3. Remove from the heat and add the butter and vanilla.
4. (Do not be concerned about the texture at this point. The blender will homogenize the sauce, making it as creamy as any chocolate sauce you might remember.) Transfer the sauce to the blender and process at cream or blend until smooth.
5. Serve warm over pancakes.

Protein
and
Mineral Charts

The following charts are to provide you with basic protein and mineral information. This information will enable you to compute the approximate nutritional value of any meal you prepare. Should you be following one of the basic recipes, but substituting flours, you can quickly determine whether that substitution has been a plus or minus on the side of protein and you can adjust accordingly. Barley used in place of wheat, for example, will yield a lower protein product so you may want to boost that protein level with wheat germ, soy flour or brewer's yeast. Likewise, there is a considerable nutritional difference between coconut and pecans, for example, and you should bear this in mind when exchanging nuts in the various recipes.

All values, except as indicated, are derived from the U.S. Department of Agriculture Handbook No. 8, "Composition of Foods, Raw, Processed, Prepared," by Bernice K. Watt and Annabel L. Merrill. It is a tremendously useful book. Perhaps the only drawback is that all values are given for 100 g. measures, so that it is necessary to compute those values for the known weight of a standard volume. The average weight for a cup of flour, for example, is 113 g., although flours range anywhere from 72 g. (full fat soy) to 140 g. (carob), as shown in the following chart, which converts 100 g. values into those for a cup of each respective flour. Nuts also vary in weight, so that while a cup of dried shredded coconut barely moves the balance at 62 g., a cup of almonds weighs in at a hefty 142 g. It is therefore important to know the weight of a food per standard volume in order to translate the 100 g. scores into readily usable information.

In the fruit chart, however, I have merely reproduced the information given in Handbook No. 8 per 100 g. measure. There is much nutritional variation with fruits, even more so than with grains. In addition to soil and cultivation differences, there is now a wide range of drying methods. Commercially prepared fruits can be dehydrated, evaporated, sulfured, unsulfured, moisturized, and/or softened. All of these have an effect on nutritional value, so at best all you can do is a comparative analysis. See if you are getting more or less potassium or vitamin A when you switch from apricot sauce to prunes. What will you gain by mixing dates with the raisins? (Niacin.) If you *must* have a standard to go by: 1/2 cup of raisins weighs 80 g.

HOME GROUND FLOURS

Grain	Protein/ 100 g	Approx. Weight/Cup	Protein/ Cup
Buckwheat, dark	11.7 g	100 g	11.7 g
Barley, light pearled	8.2	112	9.18
pot or scotch	9.6	112	10.75
Carob	4.5	140	6.4
Chickpeas (garbanzo beans)	20.5	72	14.76
Corn, yellow or white	9.2	118	10.86
Millet	9.9	113	11.2
Rice, brown	7.5	120	9.0
Rolled Oats	14.2	80	11.4
Rye, medium	12.1	119	14.4
Soy beans	34.1	72	24.6
Wheat, durum	12.7	120	15.2
hard red spring	14	120	16.8
hard red winter	12.3	120	14.8
soft red winter	10.2	113	11.52
soft white	9.4	113	10.62
Triticale*		116	14.0

* This value is based on protein information for triticale berries as given on page 543, *Laurel's Kitchen,* by Robertson, Flinders and Godfrey, Nilgiri Press: California, 1976.

NUTS AND SEEDS

1 Cup	Approx. Weight	Protein	Calcium	Phosphorus	Iron	Sodium	Potassium	Thiamin	Riboflavin	Niacin
Almonds	142 g	26.4 g	332 mg	715.7 mg	6.7 mg	5.7mg	1,098 mg	.34 mg	1.3 mg	4.97mg
Brazil	140	20	260.4	970.2	4.76	1.4	1,001	1.34	.168	2.24
Cashews	140	24.08	53.2	522.2	5.32	21	649.6	.60	.35	2.5
Coconut (un-sweetened)	62	4.5	16.1	115.9	2	—	364.6	.037	.02	.4
Filberts	140	17.6	293	472	4.8	2.8	96	.64	—	1.3
Macadamia	140	10.9	67.2	225	2.8	—	370	.48	.15	1.8
Millet	202	19.8	40	6.2	13.6	—	860	1.46	.76	4.6
Peanuts	150	39	103.5	601.5	3.2	7.5	1,011	1.71	.195	25.8
Pecans	108	9.9	78.8	312	2.6	—	651.2	.92	.14	.97
Pumpkin seed	140	40.6	71.4	1,602	15.7	—	—	.34	.27	3.36
Sesame seed	145	27	1,682	893	15.2	87	1,051	1.42	.35	7.8
Sunflower seed	145	34.8	174	1,214	10.3	43.5	1,334	2.84	.33	7.8
Walnut, Black	125	25.6	—	712	7.5	3.7	575	.28	.14	.8
Walnut, English	120	17.8	118.8	456	3.7	2.4	540	.396	.16	1.1

— Indicates that no measurable quantity of the mineral or vitamin is present.

DRIED FRUITS

100 g.	Protein	Calcium	Phosphorus	Iron	Sodium	Potassium	Vitamin A	Thiamine	Riboflavin	Niacin
Apples, dehydrated	1.4 g	40 mg	66 mg	2.0 mg	7 mg	730 mg	—	—	.06 mg	.6 mg
Apricots, dehydrated	5.6	86	139	5.3	33	1,260	14,100 mg	—	.08	3.6
Dates	2.2	59	63	3.0	1	648	50	.09 mg	.10	2.2
Figs	4.3	126	77	3.0	34	640	80	.10	.10	.7
Peaches, dehydrated	4.8	62	151	3.5	21	1,229	5,000	—	.10	7.8
Pears, dried sulfured	3.1	35	48	1.3	7	573	70	.01	.18	.6
Prunes	3.3	90	107	4.4	11	940	2,170	.12	.22	2.1
Raisins	2.5	62	101	3.5	27	763	20	.11	.08	.5

— Indicates no measurable quantity of the nutrient.

Cereal Glossary

Grains, groats, grits—there is a name for every cereal type and texture. You must know some names when purchasing ingredients.

Bolt: to sift, as for flour. In times past, this was done through a fine-meshed cloth.

Bran: the outer coating of a cereal grain, containing the majority of the cereal's fiber.

Buckwheat: the seed of the herb buckwheat, used as a cereal grain. The two varieties used as such are *Fagopyrum esculentum* and *Fagopyrum tartaricum.*

Bulghur: parched cracked wheat. The term "bulghur" has also been used to refer to any grain that has been parched and cracked.

Corn meal: a meal ground from corn. "Meal" indicates that the grind is coarse.

Couscous: this term can refer to semolina, cracked millet, cracked wheat or kasha.

Cultigen: a cultivated organism for which a wild ancestor is known. Corn is a good example.

Durum wheat: *Triticum durum* ("*durum*" being the Latin for "hard"). The flour of this species of wheat is particularly high in gluten, and is therefore excellent for yeast doughs.

Farina: a fine meal of cereal grains used mainly for breakfast cereals. It is creamy colored and made from hard, but not *durum*, wheat. The commercially prepared product can be duplicated at home with any variety of hard wheat.

Flaxseed: the seed of the herb *Linum usitatissimum,* used as a source of oil and fiber.

Frumenty: a dish of wheat boiled in milk—classically flavored with sweeteners, spices and raisins.

Germ: comprises approximately 2% of the cereal kernel and contains the highest grade protein and all of the fat.

Graham: whole wheat flour, named after Sylvester Graham, an American dietary reformer of the mid-nineteenth century. Today, the "graham" label on commercially milled flour indicates that it has been ground from hard wheat.

Groat: a grain with the hull removed (such as oat or buckwheat groats) or the hulled grain broken into fragments that are larger than grits.

Grits: any coarsely ground hulled grain. Corn (hominy) and soy grits have been precooked, dried, then cracked.

Gruel: a thin porridge.

Hard wheat: spring or winter, hard wheat varieties are the highest in protein, ranging from 14% to 24% in some Northern latitudes. The berry of hard wheat is literally harder than soft or pastry wheat and grinds to a uniformly textured tan colored flour.

Hasty pudding: in England, it is a porridge of oatmeal and flour boiled in water; in New England, it's corn meal mush.

Hominy: hulled corn with the germ removed, usually by soaking in lye water.

Hominy Grits: hominy that has been cracked or ground into granular particles.

Kasha: coarsely milled buckwheat, barley or millet.

Loblolly: a thick gruel.

Maslin: a bread made of wheat and rye flours.

Meal: coarsely ground and unbolted seeds of a cereal grass (not wheat) or pulse (legume).

Middlings: a by-product of grain milling, usually refers to wheat.

Mush: a thick porridge made with cornmeal boiled in water or milk.

Pastry Wheat: a soft wheat, usually 10% to 12% protein, used for making cakes, cookies, and other non-yeast baked goods.

Porridge: a soft food made by boiling grain or legume meal in milk or water until until thick.

Proso: *Panicum miliaceum,* or millet, a small seeded annual grass.

Pulse: the edible seeds of leguminous crops, such as peas, beans, lentils and peanuts.

Samp: cracked corn.

Semolina: creamy colored, granular, protein rich *durum* wheat flour. Sometimes it refers to the purified middlings of any hard wheat.

Sesame: the seed of the annual herb, *Sesamum indicum.*

Soft white wheat: the lowest protein wheat, also whitest in color, ranging from 8% to 10% protein. Used for baked goods requiring lightness and delicacy. Its low protein, hence low gluten content, renders it a poor choice for yeast doughs.

Spelt: a variety of wheat containing two light red kernels held in "spikelets," hence the name, *Triticum spelta.*

Water Ground: Refers to corn meal, generally. This process of milling retains the germ.

Index

Stone mills, xxi-xxii
Stove-Top Rice Cream, 167
Strawberries, 187
Streptococcus thermophilus, in yogurt, 171
Sunflower Potica, 132, 133
Sunflower seeds, 6-9, 12-14, 21-23, 43, 46,
        50, 91, 114, 132, 152-154, 161,
        166, 168, 177, 179, 194
    in granolas, 27, 31, 34, 36-39, 52-56
    heat effects on, xvii
    nutritional value of, xvi, 202
    in yeast dough, 128
Swedish Carob Cakes, 103
Swedish Cake, (Basic), 102
    variations of, 105
Swedish Corn Cakes, 104
Swedish Oat Cakes, 103
Swedish Oat Soy Cakes, 103
Swedish pancakes, 62, 100-105, 184, 187,
        189, 191, 197
Swedish Rice Cakes, 104
Swedish Wheat Soy Cakes, 103
Sweetened Yogurt, 175
Sweeteners
    for granolas, 27
    recommended, xix
Syrup, for granola squares, 57

Tahini, 15, 179
Thiamine
    in dried fruits, 203
    in nuts and seeds, 202
Timber Crest dried fruits, 191
Toppings, 184-198
Trail food, wheat germ mixes as, 43
Triple Grain Cereal, 7
Triticale, 3, 29, 168
    dough, 129
    flakes, 20
    flour, nutritional value, 201
    muffins, 135, 142, 161
    pancakes, 62, 65, 74, 76, 80, 81, 85, 105,
        118, 121
    crepes, 86, 92
Triticale Cakes, 76
100% Triticale Crepes, 92
Triticale Flake Cakes, 85
100% Triticale Muffins, 142

Vanilla, 53
Vitamin A, 18, 28, 38, 48, 178, 200
    in dried fruits, 203
Vitamins B, 40, 45, 171, 173, 178, 191
    in dried fruits, 203
    loss of, in commercial flours, xx

in nuts and seeds, 202
Vitamin C, 28
Vitamin E, rancid oils and, xx, 40
Vitamin K, 171

Walnuts, 43, 91, 114, 144, 153, 157, 159,
        166
    nutritional value of, 202
Water ground, definition of, 206
Wheat, 204, 205
    allergy to, 63, 103, 135, 141-142, 177
    berries, 3, 85, 91, 92, 95, 168, 205
        in blender pancakes, 110-115, 117,
            118
    bran, 28
    flakes, 20
    flour, xxi, 29
        home-made, xxi, 201
        nutritional value, 201
    gluten in, 119, 121
    granolas, 27, 29, 36
    muffins, 135, 137-140, 144-146, 162
    pancakes, 62, 65, 66-72, 74, 75, 77-80,
        82, 84, 85, 102, 103, 105, 106,
        108, 110-115, 118-121
    crepes, 86-90, 93, 94
    porridges, 6, 7, 12-14
    puffed, 58, 59
    red spring, 13
        protein in, xvi
    soft vs. hard, 66, 135
    in yeast dough, 124
Wheat Berry Cream, 168
Wheat Flake Cakes, 85
Wheat germ, xvi, 11, 22, 59, 60, 100, 164,
        166, 176, 177, 179, 185, 200
    bars, 45, 46-50
    cereals, 40-44
    cooking of, xvii
    in granolas, 27, 31, 32, 34-38
        bars, 51-54, 56
    muffins, 138, 143, 149
    nutritive value of, 40, 45
    pancakes, 74-75, 79, 102, 105, 112,
        118, 121
    crepes, 92
    rancid, xx
    toasting of, 40, 48
    in yeast dough, 129
Wheat Germ Crepes, 92
Wheat Germ Mixes, 43
Wheat Germ Muffins, 149
Wheat Germ Oat Cakes, 74-75
Wheat Germ Yeast Pancakes, 121
Wheat Germ Sesame Cakes, 75
Wheat Griddlecakes, 65, 66-67

NOTES

NOTES

NOTES

NOTES

NOTES

NOTES

NOTES

NOTES